# MY LIFE MY TRAVELS

*Sometimes in life... unexpectedly,*
*The end becomes a beginning...*
*My new life begins where this book ends...*

# MY LIFE MY TRAVELS

*A Travelogue*

Sundeep Bhutoria

Edited by
Mita Kapoor and Siyahi team

*My Life My Travels*

a travelogue by Sundeep Bhutoria

First impression (in English) 2016 published by
Nine Books an imprint of Vani Prakashan

Vani Prakashan
4695, 21-A Daryaganj New Delhi 110002
www.vaniprakashan.in

Translation of *Aapbeeti Jagbeeti*
published in Hindi by Rajkamal Prakashan Private Ltd.



ISBN: 978-93-5229-496-1

10 9 8 7 6 5 4 3 2 1



Design
Malay Ganguly

Printed and bound by Anderson Printing House Pvt. Ltd. Kolkata

# Contents

# *Author's Note*

This is my second visit to South Korea. Approximately one crore thirty lac people live in Seoul, the capital of this country; that is a little more than in Kolkata. We always console ourselves by saying that the root cause of all the problems in our country such as cleanliness, governance of the city, traffic, sewerage, electricity and unemployment etc. is over-population. If over-population is a hindrance to progress, South Korea has proved it wrong. The progress that Seoul has made cannot be described in words. In Seoul, you find skyscrapers like in New York and the cleanliness like in Europe fifteen years ago. Koreans have made this city extremely beautiful and organized with their hard work and dedication. People of Seoul are very punctual and the Incheon Airport of Seoul has got the title of the world's most organized airport.

When I met their Prime Minister with the Secretary General of United Nations, Ban-Ki-moon, he told me very enthusiastically that our countries had signed a very important trade agreement. India's Cabinet Minister, Mr. Anand Sharma was in the headlines of their newspapers because of the bi-lateral agreement for economic partnership.

There has not been any limit to my travels abroad in the last fifteen years. Whenever I go to a new country or city, I try to compare their life-style, civilization, traditions and discipline with those of our country. I had never thought that these stories would be published as the book that is in your hands. I used to just narrate my experiences in gatherings of friends and small, intimate groups. In one such gathering, when I was narrating my experiences abroad to the then editor of Kolkata's newspaper *Jansatta*, Mr. Shambunath Shukla, he said, "Why don't you pen down these incidents?" I thought he was joking. But, he was serious. He wanted to publish these anecdotes of foreign travels as a weekly column in his newspaper and thus *Aapbeeti Jagbeeti* was born. I wrote an article every Sunday for two years along with continuing my journeys abroad. People also liked the column because there are very few descriptions of foreign travels in Hindi. Then I got married and stopped writing. In spite of many letters and the suggestions of the editors of other Hindi newspapers, I could not write *Aapbeeti Jagbeeti* again. But my journeys abroad continue even now. Now when those columns are being compiled into a book, I am writing this piece as a window into the journey that follows.

Acharya Kalyanmal Lodha and Mr. Ramsharan Joshi had asked me many-a-time to get these anecdotes published, but I had never paid any attention. But one day when I was narrating some of my experiences of travel to Africa to the famous writer of Bangla literature, Mrs. Nabaneeta Dev Sen, she said that I must get my anecdotes published in the form of a book and thus, this book was born.

I hope that the reader would ignore the language of wanderer-like anecdotes because I do not know how to write in a literary fashion. All the anecdotes have been written in an unpolished and disorderly fashion, just like the journeys.

*Sundeep Bhutoria*
Seoul
11 August, 2009

*Translation from Aapbeeti Jagbeeti*

# *Introduction of Aapbeeti Jagbeeti*

Life in itself is an extraordinary journey but the journey of the external world is more colourful, inimitable and challenging than the internal world. All of us keep travelling from one place to another. There was a time when travelling to holy places used to be a person's last wish. Parallel to travelling for religion is travelling for exploration, preaching, business, sight-seeing etc. In modern times, the importance of travel as tourism has established itself again. A big section of the society is associated with it.

But travelling and travelling with an insight are two different things. All of us travel but how many of us can give these travels a creative expression or make them purposeful? When the narration of a journey or travelogue touches creativity, this journey becomes a part of the literary world. In short, a travelogue is a creative process of understanding familiar or unfamiliar society or region by seeing it oneself.

Young and inquisitive Sundeep Bhutoria has definitely startled me by presenting himself as an awakened and sensitive travel writer in his first travelogue *Aapbeeti Jagbeeti*. About eight years ago, I had a brief meeting with Sundeep at the residence of late Dr. Prabha Khaitan in Kolkata. At that time, I was told that Sundeep had little interest in business and he was actively involved in social activities. During the various meetings that followed, I came to know that Sundeep is also associated with different organizations related to the United Nations and keeps travelling, both within the country and abroad, in context of his work. Sundeep has an unparalleled knack for observing societies and lifestyles. The result of this observation is the present book.

It was Prabha*ji*, who had first told me that her son was a writer too and that he had also penned down anecdotes of his many travels which had been published in the Kolkata edition of *Jansatta*. First published at the start of the millennium, Sundeep's travel writings have now taken the shape of a book.

Sundeep has given words to his journey and extraordinary experiences through the different continents during the first stage of his wanderings. The speciality of Sundeep's travel writings lies in the fact that he never forgets his society, his country and his ethics. Sundeep may be in New York or Paris, in Britain or Japan, he may be travelling in the countries of South Africa or South America; Kolkata, Rajasthan and India are never separated from him. In his travelogues, a stream of comparative insight into different societies and lifestyles continues to flow. At the end of each chapter, Sundeep's pen brings out the most amazing insights that leave the reader pondering over his story.

Sundeep is primarily a businessman. But through the course of the book, the "businessman" never overshadows the "writer". This work has a collection of his travel stories that were published in the year 2002 and I hope to someday see a compilation of the subsequent stories too.

I wish Sundeep all the success on this first attempt!

*Ramsharan Joshi*

*Translation from Aapbeeti Jagbeeti*

# *Preface of Aapbeeti Jagbeeti*

One evening in the year 2002, I was looking everywhere for Sundeep Bhutoria. The week's issue of our Sunday magazine *Sabrang* was finalized and the only thing left was Sundeep's column *Aapbeeti Jagbeeti*. Sundeep was neither receiving his calls nor was he responding to any messages. At that time, I was the local editor of *Jansatta*, Kolkata. I was anxious because if Sundeep's column did not reach, it would cause embarrassment for me.

It was about eleven at night, when I received a call from Sundeep, "Yes, what is it?"

I was in a state of panic by then. "Where are you? What happened to your column?"

"I am in Japan. But the column will reach you by tomorrow morning. I have dictated the matter to my secretary." Sundeep replied calmly.

This is one of Sundeep's greatest assets. I have never seen him in haste or even agitated. Even in the moments of distress, Sundeep keeps his cool. Travelling is like an addiction for Sundeep. One can never know when Sundeep would go away to Delhi or Bengaluru while talking to you in Jaipur. He never keeps any bag or the essentials for the travel with him. He just carries one set of *kurta-pyjama* and Kolhapuri footwear; a credit card and some money in his pocket. His needs are very basic. Once I happened to meet Sundeep at Kolkata's Netaji Subhash Chandra Bose International Airport while returning from Delhi and he was not carrying anything except a mobile.

Sundeep himself says that he is not a tourist. He is a wanderer and a wanderer needs neither money nor luggage. He only needs his quest. Sundeep had first gone to London when he was twenty years old and that too, on a tourist visa. Sundeep did his post-graduation, completed a management course and took over his family business, but he did not compromise on his travels. He became the president of the Marwari Youth Federation and protested against many social evils prevalent in the society. He started a movement to stop dowry, to limit the number of guests in weddings and to end the incessant show-off.

To have a person of his stature write a column regularly was not easy but I was impressed by his style of narration and knowledge. I pleaded with his *Maa*, Dr. Prabha Khaitan that I wanted a column on Sundeep's travels every week. I knew he would never say no to her, and so wanted her to ask him to write. Prabha*ji* smiled and said, "Shukla*ji*, I cannot guarantee that Sundeep will write a column every week, but I will definitely make him write." Thus started the journey of *Aapbeeti Jagbeeti* with Sundeep Bhutoria.

Many of my colleagues protested against Sundeep's column in *Jansatta*. Some called it my dictatorship, some considered it my unfamiliarity with the land of Bengalis and others took it as an insult to all the Hindi writers of Kolkata. But I was adamant. I started Sundeep's column stopping some other columns. In Kolkata, there is a strong lobby of Hindi writers. They expelled me from Hindi community. I was no longer invited to the programmes and meetings of Hindi writers. But I benefitted from this. I got associated with the Bengali and Marwari genteel society, Punjabi association, Gujarati and South Indian society.

The reputation of the paper increased among the elite, who controlled the market. In the name of purity, the Hindi community had closeted the newspapers so tightly that no light reached there. I opened those doors and as a result, the circulation of the paper, which was merely five thousand before my joining, crossed eighty-five thousand within six months. After starting Sundeep's column, we were flooded with letters. Everyone loved it. I told Sundeep that I wanted his column to focus on his travels only. Sundeep recollected London, New York, Paris to Alimuddin Street of Kolkata in his column dauntlessly.

The owners of the newspapers and their employees treat the readers of Hindi newspapers as the wife of a poor, who would read whatever we would offer them. The editors of the Hindi newspapers decide the preference of news sitting in their air-conditioned chambers and the poor reader has to tolerate all that. Some newspapers have started publishing the leftovers from their English counterparts. These papers believe that no good material is being written in Hindi. Sundeep Bhutoria has broken these myths. He knows Hindi, English and Bangla literature quite well but he writes only in Hindi. He believes that by writing in Hindi, we can spread our views to a bigger section of our society.

*Shambhunath Shukla*
Officiating Editor, Amar Ujjala
New Delhi

*Translation from Aapbeeti Jagbeeti*

## *Introduction of Kato Rajpath, Janapad...*

A travelogue may be of various kinds. It can be a continuous story or a collection of pieces of glimpses, a subjective narrative or an objective description. I like all sorts of travel stories – holidaying, visiting a country, researching history, venturing on to the hills or into the seas, pilgrimage, educational tours and travelling while attending meetings. I am extremely fond of travel. Besides travelling myself, I like to read others' travel stories. Sundeep Bhutoria's beloved mother, Dr. Prabha Khaitan, was a poet. Sundeep also is a very good story-teller. Sometimes, he used to narrate amazing stories of various countries, leaving me spellbound. I felt an urge to share those stories with others. So, one day, I asked him, "Sundeep, why don't you write down the stories of your travels?" Sundeep smiled and said, "I do write. Many of the stories have appeared as columns in *Sabrang*."

I was happy and wanted to know if he had made them into a book. Sundeep said, "I've never thought of a book. Who will publish it? Whom can I approach?" Immediately I gave him the address of Ashok Maheswari, the publisher of my Hindi books, in Delhi, and advised Sundeep to send him the manuscript. Publication of story collections is quite in vogue in Hindi literature. And, as I expected, Rajkamal brought out Sundeep's travelogue *Aapbeeti Jagbeeti*. Readers lapped up the book and further editions were printed. At this point, I thought, why should the Bengali readers be deprived of this book, which has gained so much popularity among Hindi readers? Sundeep is not the son of Jaipur only, he belongs to Kolkata too. I told Sundeep about my thoughts. Sundeep is someone who does not need a long gestation period for implementing an idea. Very soon, I gathered that he had already got Kalipada*babu* on board as his translator and the work on the Bengali version of his book was in full swing. The next question was who would publish the book? I called Sudhangshu Dey of Dey's Publishing, who is also the publisher of my books. Dey's came forward and published Sundeep's book.

The pages of the book are filled with the light and air of many countries. There are many people, much fun, much sorrow, many histories and many unknown facts. The reader gets to connect with an educated mind full of humour and wit. Every line of this book bears testimony of a globalised era.

Sundeep's tireless travel across the globe will definitely not decrease. It will, in fact, go on increasing, thanks to both his passion and profession. The traders in ancient times, used to travel from one country to another via sea routes and bring along unknown cultures of foreign countries. Sundeep looks after his family business within the country, but his area of work is spread across the globe. His travel knows no boundaries. In his capacity in WFUNA, he travels throughout the world. He is associated with many social welfare activities, both in our country and abroad. This has given him the opportunity to have many incredible experiences.

Sundeep likes to call himself a wanderer. So, let us start looking forward to the next volume from him, while congratulating him for this one.

*Bhalobasa!*

*Nabaneeta Dev Sen*

*Translation from Kato Rajpath, Janapad...*

## *Preface of Kato Rajpath, Janapad...*

Like renowned social worker and learned Prabha Khaitan, her worthy son Sri Sundeep Bhutoria is also well-known in Bengal's cultural world and is associated with many philanthropic activities. Sundeep is the principal driving force for Pronam, a project to support the lonely, old people, that is being run under the aegis of The Bengal and with which many of us are connected. Good-looking, educated, soft-spoken and polite, Sundeep attracts one and all. Then, one day, as I got hold of the book *Aapbeeti Jagbeeti*, I came to know about the writer in him. He manages time for writing even in the midst of his pre-occupation with his family, business and social work.

A few pages into Sundeep's book, I realized it was a travelogue. The small chapters of the book had been published as a series in the newspaper *Jansatta*. I am a great fan of travelogues. I have travelled quite a lot myself. But I was surprised to find that Sundeep, though much younger to me, had been to many more countries than I had. Apart from his personal visits, he has to attend meetings at various places due to his association with some of the organizations of the United Nations.

A good travelogue is one that takes the reader on a voyage. The author does not observe alone, he takes the readers with him on his travels. Whatever he is seeing, his surprises and thrills get reflected on the readers' minds. A true traveller does not only see the famous places, he observes nature's beauty and the life experiences of the people unknown. Sheer description does not make a true travelogue; minute observation of the traveller gives it the ticket to the world of literature. Some amount of history, culture and social reality should be there in the stories. But there should be a cautious restraint so that a travel story does not become an article.

Sundeep's stories satisfy most of these conditions. However, the stories are rather brief, as they were meant for newspaper columns, every story stops short of giving the reader a sense of complete satisfaction and he tends to long for more. Such a sense of dissatisfaction is a good sign as it points to the fact that the stories are not monotonous or dull.

Let me mention here an interesting anecdote. Sundeep is a vegetarian by family tradition. Being a vegetarian often puts one through a great deal of trouble in western countries. In South American countries, especially Brazil and Argentina, where animal food comprises staple diet, most people do not even know the meaning of vegetarianism. While travelling through those countries, Sundeep got weary of lack of adequate vegetarian food. In one place he writes: "I came to a much more difficult situation at the time of visiting Peru's ancient civilization Machu-Picchu. When I did not get anything except apples for two days, I bought a vegetarian sandwich, removed the pieces of fish, washed it clean with milk and ate the bread. Whatever it takes to survive is preferable to death."

A thrilling chapter in the book is the one on the horrific incident of 9/11 in New York; a suicide terror attack that destroyed the famous twin towers, killing and injuring thousands. Sundeep Bhutoria was in New York that day and escaped miraculously.

The Bengali translation of the book has been done by Kalipada Das. It is an easy and lucid translation that is a smooth read. His command over both the languages, Bengali and Hindi, has made the translation both accurate and a pleasure to read. I strongly believe that travel-loving Bengalis will like the book very much. Sundeep should not stop his writing, we want more from him.

*(Late) Sunil Gangopadhyay*

*Translation from Kato Rajpath, Janapad...*

## *Few words on Kato Rajpath, Janapad...*

I have travelled across the globe, but my experiences are not the same as those of Sundeep. I have also penned quite a lot of travelogues, but the humanism and the love for people across boundaries revealed in his book is missing in my writings.

I read the Bengali translation of Sundeep Bhutoria's *Aapbeeti Jagbeeti* and have really appreciated the book. Sundeep is a very dear friend and I wish large circulation and success for the book.

*Buddhadev Guha*

I had heard that Sri Sundeep Bhutoria had compiled his experiences of travelling across the world and was thrilled to get the Bengali translation of those essays. Sundeep's expression is so amazing that reading through his experiences I feel as if I was with him on all those journeys. At the same time, I realize that I would not have been able to see things the way he did. His instincts served as an extra pair of eyes for him.

In his writings, Sundeep has captured each country with its own character and distinction. The nature, environment and surroundings of a country show up with vivid clarity. The society and people appear with their own distinctive features. Sundeep's description shows his sense of restraint, wit, humour and, at times, turns critical.

It is only when the writer's vision and thoughts are clear to himself that his language becomes revealing. Sundeep has never forgotten his own self and has always remembered his roots. At the same time, he has not overly thrust himself upon his narration, even while maintaining a subjective style.

Pieces from poems written by famed poets peep out from the flowing incidents, nature and characters of the countries travelled. This feels like tiny jewels lying on the grass fields.

There is more than judgment and observation that characterizes Sundeep's vision. There is a touch of poetry. In one instance, he describes a vast landscape with the metaphor of a 'sea of land'.

My thanks and good wishes to Sundeep for giving me the opportunity to read this book.

*Joy Goswami*

Sundeep Bhutoria's *Aapbeeti Jagbeeti* has been widely accepted by the Hindi-and-Bengali-speaking fraternity.

This is an astounding travelogue. I am very delighted to have had a chance to read it. Bengali readers have a deep fascination for travel and keen interest in reading travel literature.

I wish the book is widely read and the initiative meets every success.

My good wishes and blessings.

*Mahasweta Devi*

Above are the English translations of Bengali praises on *Kato Rajpath, Janapad...* (Bengali translated version of *Aapbeeti Jagbeeti*) published by Dey's publishing in 2012.

# Foreword

As we step into another new dawn of another year, we pledge, again, to make ourselves better human beings, to provide not only for our own but also for others, less privileged than us. And thus begins yet another preparation for our lives ahead. Like most of you, I too thought a great deal about the process of preparation, I even called my Acting School: An Actor Prepares! But for me, the meaning of preparation underwent a change. It evolved into the immediate and now, it transformed from planning to acting, from dreaming into living the dream. From my earliest days in Shimla, my father instilled a sense of purpose in me and my brother. It was unconventional thinking out-of-the-box and this great philosophy prepared me for my life as an actor that came with its insecurities and heartbreak. My first film, *Saraansh*, gave me fame, recognition, a little money but most significantly, the reputation of an actor.

I had earlier studied at NSD, the renowned institution where actors were initiated into acting and I came away having imbibed much, yet the process was not quite over with the course. What I benefitted most from, was watching others, being sensitive to their body language, their nuances, their eccentricities that marked them apart as individuals. Travelling was a part of this learning curve. I distinctly recollect my first visit to London, for a shoot, in the early years. So exhilarated and excited I was that I stood on a makeshift stool in Leicester Square and sang old Hindi film songs to an audience who applauded with delight at this impromptu performance by a young Indian man. It makes me smile when I walk past the same spot, often to a premiere of one of my films in the cinema hall there. Life teaches you so much when you live in the moment.

Sundeep Bhutoria has done just that with *Aapbeeti Jagbeeti*. He has travelled and experienced the adventures life has offered him with open arms. I hope readers take a page from his book and live each day to its fullest, embrace the dawn with hope and optimism.

Best Wishes

*Anupam Kher*

# MY LIFE MY TRAVELS

# Passing Through Many Continents

I recall reading the phrase *Jo ramta nahi, wo Ram nahi* in *Are Yayavar Rahega Yaad* by Agyeya, during grade ten. Ramna means travelling and Ram stands for Maryada Purshottam Ram.[1] In other words, to be an ideal person according to Indian traditions, one must travel. I understand the literal meaning of the phrase now, when I have seen it all, from expediting the forests of Africa, to visiting Tokyo's luminous buildings, sailing across the Atlantic Ocean and witnessing the never-ending nights of Scandinavian countries. During my travels, I have understood various codes of conduct and experienced their construction and deconstruction, truth and falsehood, preservation and destruction of cultures.

Rajendra Yadav, in his autobiography *Mud Mud Ke Dekhta Hu*, says, "I don't know why, when I hear others narrating their experiences or read them in books, I don't remember anything… I forget my surroundings… I sense only myself and my experiences brimming within it or an incident from my life, absolutely irrelevant to the narrator." This applies to me as well.

My acquaintances often ask me for advice on how to go to a specific place, what one needs to do, how the experience would be or what my experience has been, etc. Having moved six times by the time I completed tenth grade, I received my education in cities situated on the banks of the Ganges and the Yamuna. I first travelled outside India in 1994. I had left for seven days but returned after about thirteen months. Since then, I have visited more than fifty countries. My travel hasn't been limited to tourist spots such as the Statue of Liberty in New York or the Buckingham Palace in London. I have extensively studied the lifestyle, civilization, culture and ethos of various countries. For the last seven years, I have been out of Kolkata for about ten days a month, either on business or to carry out my responsibilities towards the associations I am involved with. Due to my globe-trotting expeditions, my friends often joke that I live out of a suitcase.

Except for the Hanging Gardens of Babylon and the Pyramids of Egypt, I don't recall any place that I haven't visited. As far as travel is concerned, Athens is the only city left for me to explore. During my tours, I have not only met great people like Margaret Thatcher, Yasser Arafat, Michael Jackson, Vladimir Putin, Bill Gates, Demi Moore, Nelson Mandela and Kofi Annan but also brought back memories of strangers and friendships I'll cherish forever.

So I thought, why not share the tales of my travels, amusing instances and memorable moments that have both, the depth of oceans and the vastness of the skies, friendly strangers and evasive friends and relatives? The chronicles have the awe of Egypt's Pyramids, the darkness of Tanzanian forests, the chill of Siberia, glamorous dazzle of Hollywood, the modernity of the West and conventions of the Gulf countries. It would include not only pleasant evenings in London and the suffocating weather of Copenhagen but also give you a glimpse of Spain's beauty and shopping in Singapore.

These anecdotes include a few unforgettable experiences of narrow escapes from death witnessing its destructive dance. Let me take you to France's Monte Carlo and Nice with sea waves crashing on their shores and the biting cold Jungfrau Mountains of Switzerland with their sad silence of formality and exuberance of frankness.

[6 January, 2002]

[1]Sobriquet given to Lord Ram symbolizing the best behaved among men

# Ruins Do Tell

When I was a child, I couldn't understand how the earth revolves round the sun and how the imaginary lines of latitude and longitude are marked. I used to argue in class that if the earth is one, how can there be day in India and night in America. How can one prove that time in London is about five hours behind or ahead of time here? I could never figure it out.

When I was in primary school, the geography classes at schools in the small suburb of Sujangarh were not equipped with maps or videos. According to a scholar - 'We cannot find truth. We can only sense its presence through the mirror of our illusions.' One day I understood that without going around the world, without experiencing it, I will not be able to sense the reality of this notional geography.

I was planning to go to another country to attend a wedding. Till then I was not aware of the formalities of getting a visa, though I knew about the requirement of a passport for travelling abroad. It took a lot of time to get the consent of my family. In a family of nearly a hundred, neither had anyone ever been abroad and nor did anyone ever think of it. While Papa feared that I would go astray in London or become a non-vegetarian; Mummy was anxious that I would marry a Caucasian. So, to stop me from going, they cited my grandmother's health. After a lot of persuading and swearing by three oaths for Mummy's sake- that I would not touch alcohol and cigarettes; that I would keep my distance from girls; and that I would return soon, I finally got the consent of the family due to her efforts.

A month before the wedding, I got to know that the procedure of getting a visa may require three to four months. But I was determined. For getting the passport done, I pestered our family friend and State Home

Minister at that time, Rajesh Pilot to the clerk at the passport department, day in and day out. During those three days of getting my passport and visa, I was very restless.

I flew from Kolkata by Russian Airlines, staying in Moscow for over seven hours, before taking a plane to London. When a Russian stewardess wished me `Good Morning' while handing me a towel, I realized that the plane was about to land at Moscow. Lifting the shutter of the window, I saw hundreds of planes, parked on the runway at the Moscow airport. By that time, Russia had been divided. Later, I was informed that all those planes were owned by Aeroflot Airlines, which was once one of the world's major air services and had gone to Russia during partition. About seventy percent of the planes were not being used. Sixty percent of the airport was closed. At many places, the police was instructing the passengers through gestures not to go to the closed area. Even on that severely cold morning, there was no tea or coffee available anywhere in the airport. There were big coffee houses. Even the rate lists were hanging outside, but every place was closed. People had an unusual expression of sadness and painful silence.

I happened to glance at a chandelier. I had never seen such a grand chandelier before. I could not take my eyes off it. But there were no lights burning in it. More than half the taps in the toilets were broken. Except for one or two, none of them had any water. There was neither any enquiry office nor any kiosk of newspapers and magazines. It was definitely not the Moscow that I had heard or read about. I recalled Henry Ford's quote 'history is nonsense'. What we call development in history destroys history itself.

While boarding the plane for London, I decided to come back and see this new facet of Moscow, which Russia might never have imagined.

When the plane took off for Heathrow, London, I thought of the deserted airport and muttered, 'Ruins do tell – the building was once grand.'

[13 January, 2002]

# The Kingdom Where the Sun Never Set

While recollecting these instances, at times my thoughts stray to the misery of Moscow and at other times, they dwell on the Sethia House, situated at 32, Fitzalan Road in London. The house held the atmosphere of a wedding: people coming and going, many new faces including London's well- known NRIs, relatives and a number of guests from India. I had heard quite a lot about all those NRIs I met, such as Lord Bagri, Lord Swraj Paul, Laxmi Mall Singhvi, and Hinduja Brothers. All of them had come to attend the wedding.

Where was I in this crowd? Which streets of London was I walking? What did the icy- cold breeze from the Atlantic Ocean convey to me?

The weather in London is always damp. No one can tell when it will rain nor can anyone predict when the sun would start shining. I would put on layers of clothing – a thermal, then a t-shirt, a shirt, a half-sleeved sweater and a coat. While going out, I would put on an overcoat. As the weather changes and the day's temperature increases, one has to start taking off the clothes one by one thus increasing the weight of the bag. I would have trouble. Do I take care of myself or the sweater or the coat? Or take out the bus fare from my wallet? I felt completely lost.

Pradeep Damani, who had come from Kolkata for photographing the wedding and the spiritual singer, Rajendra Jain were also with me. Everyday Pradeep would visit one place or the other and every evening, he would narrate some unusual experience and suggest the less expensive ways of living in London. Anyway, what did I see in London? I had created a mental picture of London on the basis of what I had heard about it and when I visited those places, all I could say was, 'Yes! That's the famous Buckingham Palace. I had seen the guard of Buckingham Palace changing in many films and this is London's museum, where Karl Marx is believed to have written his famed *Das Kapital*'. The Kohinoor diamond was also locked there. I was distressed that I had to spend fifteen hundred rupees for the ticket to see what once was ours. I remember distinctly that after visiting the museum, I wrote in the suggestion book that at least Indians should be allowed to see the diamond for free or at discounted rates. I visited the famous Oxford Street. Such sparkling shops! I recalled the bioscope at *Gangaur* fair which I'd watched as a child, with recordings of 'Here comes the Empress of London! Welcome the King of Paris! Let's hear it from the maiden of Italy!'

While walking on Oxford Street, I became nostalgic for the days when *Teej* and *Gangaur* fairs were held with such breathtaking exuberance. In which corner of the past is my Rajasthan, that small suburb of Sujangarh and my uncle's house in Churu? London seemed lustreless in comparison, a result of financial crisis. First, I glimpsed a ruined Moscow and now, London. Mumbai and Delhi seemed better.

Where are the Caucasians in London? Asians everywhere! They have their own localities and shops. Every community is grouped into a separate continent altogether. How is the British government going to handle them in the future? People have settled here from all over the world! There are refugees, traders, who have come of their own will and minorities, who have suffered in their own countries. In spite of the strictness, the English have been compelled to allow them to settle. Besides, the British themselves have gone away to Canada, America or Australia. They call themselves Europeans.

Sitting on a bench in Hyde Park, I thought, London is the capital city of the once majestic British Empire where the sun never set.

[20 January, 2002]

# From the Banks of the Thames

Southall is one of the localities in London that is called 'mini Hindustan'. Even Pakistanis, who are very similar to Indians in looks, habits, conversation do not hesitate in calling themselves refugees, having run away to London during the Partition. I met Mirza Khursheed during the initial days of my stay. He lived in Sutton, the outer part of London. Earlier, he had lived in Delhi. He traded in textiles and spices. He had been associated with many social and cultural associations of Delhi. During the Partition, his family had fled India and settled in London. He had scoffed, "Whether Pakistan was formed or the British ruled the land, how did it make a difference? And now, if the Congress party of Gandhi-Nehru succession is ruling India, has it affected positive change in the country? If Zia-ul-Haq acquired power by assassinating Bhutto, did the fate of Pakistan change? Nothing is going to change anywhere!"

I used to listen to his stories sitting at the bar at the Hilton. Placing a fistful of currency on the table, he would say, "Son, as long as you have this, everything is fine, everything will be all right."

Even today his inebriated voice rings in my ears, "As long as you have this, everything is fine, and everything will be all right." I felt like asking, "What will be all right? You never carried out your share of the partnership anywhere. Now, if a problem arises in Britain, you will carry your wealth to another corner of the earth. You will always be welcome in South America, Australia, Singapore or Channel Islands. But your feet don't touch the ground anywhere. You do not belong to anyone, no one belongs to you. What stillness is this? The eyes of your wife and your children look desolate." I should have shaken him up; pulled his hair; looked straight into his eyes and asked him, "Why do people like you take so much from the earth and never give anything back? I am not against you living in London but at least do something for the people here. They have societal problems, pain and suffering here as well. Do something for them." I was infuriated.

The coffee houses and pubs of London are delightful. In spite of the fact that I don't consume alcohol, I would visit pubs and sit there sipping fresh lime. I would enter India Tea House and look around for familiar faces, reminiscing about Sardar*ji*'s tea stall or Flury's in Kolkata or Elgin Road or Maharani tea of Lansdowne, before realizing that I'm alone, here in London. The tea that you get for Rs. 1700 during the afternoon tea in London's famous tea house, Hotel Savoy never had the flavour of the tea from those tea shops of Kolkata.

Luckily, I found a vacant table in India Tea House, from where I had an easy access to the outside view. I counted my money and placed an order for a tea and a *samosa*[2] . Indians always look for *samosas*, whichever corner of the world they are in. In front of the Euston tube station, in a lane, you could find Indian, Pakistani and Bangladeshi restaurants in a row. London's famous Indian sweetmeat store, Gupta Brothers' shop is situated in the same lane. The store sold *samosas* and Calcutta *paans* in great abundance.

I recalled an incident I had read in *Freedom at Midnight*. Sir Cyril Radcliffe had drawn crooked lines on the map without consideration, dividing India and Pakistan geographically. Radcliffe had no time to visit the boundaries and consider the division from every angle before the Partition. Was this the reason for those atrocious communal killings? The British are responsible for the lingering agony of the Partition, due to which even today the gap between the two countries has not bridged. Tony Blair was now visiting the two countries to build friendly relations, but how can we forget that his ancestors' rule is responsible for shelling on the borders of the two countries quite frequently. Who knows how long it will take to heal this wound. But time is almighty and the Thames is witness to this.

[3 February, 2002]

[2] A fried triangular patty filled with vegetables, mainly boiled potatoes

# A City Run by Machines

London is a Mecca[3] for non-resident Indians. I was returning from a night club *Hippodrome* in Piccadilly, on a Sunday morning in October, at 3:30 AM. I boarded a bus for Finchley Central to go to Fitzalan Road. After getting off the bus, I had to walk about half a kilometre. One side of Fitzalan Road was lined with bungalows and on the opposite side there was a huge open ground covered with green grass. I used to walk home along a footpath situated on this huge field.

I was scared that night. The moment I took a step, a bulb of a roadside lamp lit up. I was alarmed and started running. But the automatic switching off and on of the lamp posts continued. Whichever lamp post I neared, its lamp would light up and the moment I passed it by, it would switch off and the next lamp would light up. I was sweating profusely even in the cold. Hiding my face between my knees I sat behind a roadside bench. In the morning, around six o'clock, when I saw a milkman, I called him and requested him to accompany me to my home. He used to deliver bottled milk to our home. When he heard the incident, he was in stitches. He told me that those lamp posts were automated. When a shadow fell on them, the bulbs lit up for a set time limit and they switched off again once the shadow was gone. London is a city of such automated things, automated society and automated people.

Once, at midnight, I was hungry and went down to the kitchen to look for something to eat, when a security alarm went off. Within fifteen minutes, Scotland Yard had surrounded my house. In London, if you turn on a switch and someone moves anywhere in your house except in the bedrooms, your house address flashes on the screen of the nearest police station and the alarm starts ringing. This switch is positioned outside the master bedroom. People switch it on before going to bed and switch it off in the morning. If anyone tries to break into the house, the police are automatically informed. Such is the city situated on the banks of the Thames. Tourists and non-resident Indians have such experiences quite frequently. Such incidents benefit some and harm the others.

Another time, when I was in London, plague was rampant in Surat, India. All the British airline companies had cancelled their flights to India. I was walking towards Piccadilly Road from Hotel Savoy. I was late for an appointment. The Aeroflot headquarters was on my way. I heard someone calling, 'Sundeep! Aren't you Sundeep?' Turning around, I saw the editors of a Kolkata newspaper *Jan Sansaar*, Geetesh Sharma and Kusum Jain. We were delighted to have bumped into each other, so far away from home.

Geetesh looked anxious. His flight to Kolkata had been cancelled and they weren't certain when the next flight would be scheduled. The Aeroflot employees were unable to help them. The only solution the manager gave was that Geetesh could wait there till the air services resumed or take a flight to Bangkok or Kathmandu. But Geetesh didn't agree with any of these options and there was no other way out.

I left for my appointment. Geetesh was hurt because I hadn't offered to take him out for tea. But I couldn't help it. Besides, I had to reach in time for the appointment. Nevertheless, I gave him my contact number.

[10 February, 2002]

[3] Religious place of Muslims, (here) ultimate destination

# The British Parliament Reminded Me of Churchill

Londoners still get goose bumps thinking of that fire of 1666, which burnt the whole city. The fire had started in a bakery in the Pudding Lane near London Bridge. A monument was made near the Monument Tube Station in London in memory of the people burnt in that fire. The speciality of this monument is that it is two hundred and twenty two feet tall and its distance from the bakery, where the fire had started, is also two hundred and twenty two feet.

When the British Parliament was being re-constructed after having been burnt completely, countries from all over the world sent various things to help re-build it. All these things were used in the construction of the Parliament. Very few people know that the door of the British Parliament was sent from India. It is a matter of pride that the British, who ruled us once, today, pass through a door made in our country to decide the future of theirs.

It is said that the functioning of Indian Parliament and Constitution are similar to that of the British Parliament and Constitution. The modern India that we live in today is to a great extent, a gift of the British. We are indebted to them in many ways for the structure of present day India. If the British had not invaded us, perhaps even today we would not have been able to escape the clutches of kings and landlords and priests and clerics. Before the British rule, freedom and servitude were synonymous to most Indians. It might sound as though I am going easy on the British, but rationally speaking, one should look at both sides.

Looking at the Parliament, I was reminded of one of Britain's most famous leaders, Winston Churchill, who as the Prime Minister gave a new direction to the development of Britain. Once during a debate, a woman from the opposition party told Churchill that if she were his wife, she would have poisoned him; Churchill, as his usual witty self, responded that if he were her husband, he himself would have taken the poison.

To the left of the mighty British Parliament building, is the river Thames and in front is the Waterloo Station. When I saw the Thames for the first time, I felt as if I were looking at the Hooghly from the Howrah Bridge. But the bridge on the Hooghly is bigger than that on the Thames. The banks of the river Thames serve as one of the hotspots of art, literature and culture in London and one can see people milling around enjoying tea and coffee over spirited conversations. The similarities between London and Kolkata were profound and I could understand why people referred to Kolkata as the Indian version of London.

Walking on the banks of the Thames, my mind was full of conflict. There was no time here for reflection and reminiscences. But I had come to London to understand the history of my country; to understand the heritage that these foreigners had interlaced with ours. I wanted to understand the rebellion that sent them back to their country from their point of view. At times, I think whether the so-called Independence struggle and the ensuing victory that is written about in golden letters was a result of the collective struggle or if every individual's struggle, his resistance and his desire for freedom were his own.

The banks of Thames were crowded with people and yet I felt isolated. I wasn't able to reach out to anyone. Among all those suave faces, I felt lonely. I had no friends here with whom I could share my experiences. There was no one, whose words would encourage me. In my profound loneliness, I would often stand for hours together on the shores of the Thames, searching for attachment and responsibility.

[17 February, 2002]

# Intent of 'Free Fund' Brings Notoriety

It is the youngsters who are most addicted to "free fund"[4], the Indian slang for getting things free of cost but in today's world, everyone is young as far as the attraction to free fund is concerned and the reactionary forces take full advantage of this weakness. We Indians were always taught that we should not accept anything for free from anyone. Manohar Shyam Joshi, in his book *21st Century* wrote, "Perhaps it is the proof of our being too modern and Americanized that all people who are not able to get material goods for free, are being considered indolent." Today, if one refuses to accept a freebie, his self-respect is termed as foolishness.

In foreign countries, citizens of Indian origin, particularly the tourists are notoriously known for this habit. We often read in the newspapers that someone was caught shop-lifting in some departmental store. And it is not just about shop-lifting, taking maximum benefit of something, getting one's work done, even at the cost of another person are perhaps considered a birthright by us Indians!

There are some Scandinavian and European countries, which provide basic amenities (house, car, etc.) to every citizen. In these countries, I came across many such people, who were taking undue advantage of this law. If there were three members in a family, all three would have taken home loans by cheating the government. The situation is particularly extreme in London's Southall area. There, many Punjabis had opened businesses, promising to help one acquire British citizenship. The idea was that first, they would get you to marry a British citizen and apply for your citizenship on the basis of the marriage law. Once you got the citizenship, they would get you a divorce, thus charging thousands of pounds as fee. This went on for quite some time until the government was forced to amend the law to the effect that one would have to live with his or her partner for at least a year after marriage for their citizenship to be considered.

My American friends once told me that until a few years ago, for an American student coming to India the most valuable gift from his friend would be the friend's credit card. This was the time when the world's banking system was not yet interlinked. The American student would give his credit card to a student coming to India just before his flight. Before this student landed in India, the student who was in America would report the loss of his credit card to the card company. Thus the liability of the card holder was over, but it would still be at least fifteen-sixteen hours before the card was cancelled. Taking advantage of this, the student reaching India would shop using that card, all of which would be completely free.

Another friend told me that when he was studying in America, he used to tie a wire to a one-dollar coin by making a hole in it. He would then talk for hours at the telephone booth using the same coin over and over again.

I particularly remember one embarrassing incident. While strolling at the Sharjah airport, I heard someone say, *Mera Bharat Mahaan*! On turning around, I saw an Indian employee of Sharjah airport taking out coins from a vending machine. Sensing my stare, he angrily said, "Because of you travellers, Indians everywhere gain notoriety." On asking what the matter was, I found out that these vending machines, from which one could buy cold drinks, beer, milk bottles, chocolates, snacks, cheese etc. by inserting coins, are programmed to guess the value of the coins by their weight. The weight of a forty dirham[5] coin is equivalent to the old one rupee coin. The Indians could obviously not forego this golden opportunity of getting goods worth forty dirhams for just one rupee! As a result, when on the weekends, the machine was opened, along with dirhams the workers would find one rupee coins with inscriptions of *Satyamev Jayate*[6] and there was no question on who would have put those coins in the vending machines.

[24 February, 2002]

[4] Slang used in India

[5] Sharjah uses Dirham as its official currency

[6] 'Truth always triumphs' Indian motto engraved and printed on Indian coins and currency respectively as well as put up in Indian Parliament and all government offices

# The Land of the Rising Sun

Japan is the country that receives the first rays of sunlight every morning. The local name for Japan is Nippon which is Japanese for "the rising sun". Most parts of this country receive sunlight for as long as seventeen-eighteen hours a day. Honshu, Hokkaido, Kyushu and Shikoku are the four islands which together form Japan, with Honshu and Hokkaido being the more important ones. The other two islands are comparatively far less populated. Japan has three main cities-Tokyo, Osaka and Kyoto. The Royal family of Japan lives in Kyoto which was the old capital of Nippon. Japan has a total land area of three hundred and seventy-eight thousand square kilometres, of which sixty percent is hilly and infertile, twenty-two percent is devoted to farming and the remaining eighteen percent for everything else, i.e. habitation, industry, roads, trade, etc. I have been told that in spite of the small land area, Japan is the most productive country of the world with an output of approximately $16.9 million per square kilometre as compared to America's $8.2 million. The density of population in Japan at fifteen hundred people per square kilometre is significantly more than any other country with a strong economy. With an average income of $35000, Japan is the world's richest nation today.

Being largely Buddhist, many customs and social systems of the Japanese resemble those of our own country. They too have the tradition of removing their shoes outside the house. It is a patriarchal society much like ours. The women tend not to work after marriage and rather look after the household. The Japanese do not hug or shake hands but greet each other by bowing. One who bows lower and more number of times is considered to be more polite.

In spite of Japan being the wealthiest nation of the world, people are not the wealthiest. I heard that according to Japanese law, if a person earns more than one million dollars, he has to pay eighty-eight percent of it as tax. Average saving per family is $220,000. There is so much money that the banks pay only 0.01% interests on deposits. The industrial organizations of Japan owe their success to the large cash deposits. For instance, Honda, the famous car company has a bank balance of more than fifteen billion dollars.

The self-confidence and resourcefulness of the Japanese is exceptional. Matsushita, the founder of Matsushita Electronics Ltd., the company that makes Panasonic and National electronic items, studied only till the eighth standard. After his father's death, he went to Osaka from Kyoto to earn his living. After marriage, he along with his wife and brother-in-law laid the foundation of this company. This brother-in-law of Matsushita also laid the foundation of another company that came to be known as Sanyo. At the age of ninety, when Matsushita was asked the secret of his success, his response was, "Lack of education and my never-say-die attitude!"

It is many such spirited people that inhabit the Japanese islands. It is a well-known saying that God helps those, who help themselves. There is no doubt that the future of this bright country will be even brighter. And why shouldn't it be so, when the sun also spreads its first rays of light on this country!

[3 March, 2002]

# This Form of Buddhism

Kyoto is the historical capital city of Japan. With violet hills and breath-taking views, this city situated at the heart of Japan, is known as the Magic City. The streets and lanes take you on a tour of Japanese history - houses, ambience, shrines and Buddhist temples. A shrine is the name given to temples in Japan. At many places, shrines and Buddha temples are made side by side. Seventy five percent of the population visits both the shrines and the Buddha temples.

At the Kiyomizu temple, one of the most famous temples and shrines of Japan, the Buddha idol is placed in the same compound as the Jishu Shrine. The climb up the hillock of Kiyomizu reminded me of my trips to the many hill-top temples of our country. Even the rituals followed in this temple remind you of Indian temples. Devotees have been coming here for the past thirteen hundred years to fulfil their wishes. They believe that Jishu Shrine is the god of love and relationships. The shrine is believed to help reunite lovers.

Behind the main temple building, a pair of stones is placed ten metres apart, facing each other. These stones are called "love stones". It is believed that if a person can walk from one stone to the other without falling anywhere, with closed eyes while humming their lover's name, they will get their love. At minus four degrees temperature, the crowd gathered to walk with their eyes closed is indeed a sight to behold. After one's prayer is answered, they can express their gratitude by writing their name on a small wooden slate and put it up on the adjacent wall. This wall has slates written in almost all the languages of the world.

Various kinds of talismans can also be bought, sold and tied here. There are talismans to have a successful marriage, to get one's love, to be reunited with loved ones, to have a good health, to pass an examination, to make profit in a business, to harm one's enemy as well as to beget a healthy child. But I did not see any talisman to have a male child as are found in our country. There is a separate space provided to tie the talismans. To the left of this wall of talismans and wooden slates is kept a metal idol. It is believed that an afflicted body part can be cured of pain or disease by caressing the same spot on the idol. Seeing a Japanese man caressing the idol's throat made me laugh. Once earlier, I also laughed when in Ramdevra, I saw a man with stomach ache caressing the stomach of Baba Ramdev*ji*'s statue.

I felt proud that Lord Buddha and Buddhism were India's gift to Japan. But my illusion was shattered in a couple of hours when I went to see the archeologically significant Nakiyaza temple. The priest of this Buddhist temple told me in no simpler words that there is neither any originator of Buddhism nor any God; in fact Buddhism is the adoption of a system of philosophy according to one's convenience. The priest told me that Buddha only explained the form of Buddhism. Out of regard for his status, I did not argue with the priest. Or his broken English and my little knowledge of Japanese might have brought out some other relevance of Buddhism.

It is absolutely true that Buddhism is a system of philosophy but Japan is getting disinclined to the religion it abided with. People keep changing the principles of religion according to their convenience. Buddhism is accepted here, only, as a rule of living. Above all, the Japanese accept that the biggest tenet of Buddhism is that change is constant.

[10 March 2002]

# Where Will a Human Being Be?

The second most important city of Japan, after Tokyo, is Osaka. Japan's renowned industrial units are established around this city. When I had first visited Japan, I did not get an opportunity to visit Osaka. But in February 2002, I got the chance to spend three weeks there. The organization that had invited me to Osaka had organized lectures by eminent speakers in the mornings and industry visits in the evenings.

On the first day, we were taken to famous Asahi Beer Company. This company produces twelve hundred thousand bottles of beer every day manned by a force of two hundred and thirty-one employees including the security guard and the managing director. Thousands of bottles pass through machines, beer is poured in the bottles, the bottles corked and then automatically packed into cartons – everything was done with extreme precision. The entire process was completely computerized.

Japanese industrial units have dedicated departments to handle visitors. These departments have designated employees to show the visitors the various sections of the establishment, while narrating the rich and glorious past of their companies. The famous Matsushita Electronics Ltd. that founded Panasonic and National brands has created a complete museum, House of History to commemorate the celebrated life of its founder, Matsushita. The House of History depicts every significant moment in the company's sixty-year long history along with the significant incidents of Matsushita's life in detail. Every company has elaborate arrangements to look after its visitors. The Asahi Beer Company went to the extent of providing free beer to all its visitors.

There is no doubt that Japan has made great progress in electronics. I was awestruck with the auto-pilot trains, video cameras the size of *paan*-

*parag*[7] boxes, match-box size music systems and many other such items. Everyday new goods are made, new formulae are invented. Japan was not satisfied with just mobile phones and palmtops. Bio-technology and neo-technology are rapidly being developed. I was surprised to hear an example given by a professor, while he was explaining the term 'bio'. He said that in a few years, tablets or capsules that could be split in the body through remotes would be available. The argument was that when you take a pill for an ailment, it works on the whole body equally and less than ten percent of the medicine reaches the part actually afflicted by pain. Hence, after a person has swallowed the pill, it will be taken to the part of the body that requires it using remote control technology and will be split there so that the complete benefit of the medicine reaches that part. This will apply to all medicines including everyday pills like those for ordinary fever or cold.

In some parts of Tokyo, a facility known as house convenience system was being provided that was to be available in other places soon. Under this system, you would be able to control your house from a distance of up to three hundred kilometres through your mobile. Everything would just be a button away - boiling milk, cooking, ironing clothes. You would even be able to bathe your dogs by just pressing buttons on your mobile. All this for only a few hundred American dollars. Even after seeing all this with my own eyes, I could not believe it. Such was the sheer brilliance of neo-technology.

Having seen all this, I was compelled to think whether so much progress was appropriate. Was it right to fight against nature? Will we see such a day when we would be able to change even the weather with a remote? It is great that Japan will earn three hundred billion dollars in the coming year through neo and biotechnology as per statistics, but what will happen to man? Where will the human beings be? What will happen to the human mind when even thinking will be done by machines?

[17 March, 2002]

[7] Brand name of chewing tobacco mixed with many other ingredients

# Tandoori in Japan

In Japan, Indian *tandoori*[8] food is very famous. You can find Indian restaurants everywhere, in Tokyo, Osaka, Nagoya or Kyoto. Interestingly, you hardly ever find any Indians in these so-called Indian restaurants. Usually when I am in a foreign country, I go to Indian restaurants in the evening, expecting to meet someone who speaks my language. But I did not see any Indian on the four evenings that I spent in Osaka's *Khajuraho* and *Delhi* restaurants.

I was amazed to find out that unlike in Europe or America, you do not see any Indians on the tube or in other public place in Japan. During my twenty-two day stay in Japan, the only non-resident Indians I saw were a few at the Indian Embassy. I found it ironical that even the assistant of Ramesh Singh, the owner of the *Khajuraho* restaurant in Osaka, was Japanese.

One evening, while strolling through the Sake Naakuarea in Nagoya city, I happened to see a Pakistani flag hoisted in a lane across the road. I thought it might be an office of the Pakistan Embassy, but as this flag fluttered in the breeze, on its reverse side I saw our tricolour. My curiosity piqued as I crossed the road. Entering the lane, I saw that flag having the colours of the two countries on either side, hoisted on top of a restaurant named *Gandhi*. I decided to spend the evening there and went into the restaurant hoping to meet some Indians. On entering, I was greeted by the now familiar sight of only a few Japanese and two Italians. The owner, Rafeeq Mengrani, welcomed me in traditional Japanese style and while talking to him, I learnt that he had come to Japan two years ago from Pakistan. Seeing Rafeeq talking to an Indian looking man, the cook, Mangal Gujaar came out. He had migrated to Japan from a small village in Rajasthan's Sikar district. When I told him that I also belonged to Rajasthan, his eyes sparkled with happiness. He told me that he had been in Japan for the past seven years and by now had almost forgotten his native language. He had migrated there to give his children good education and a higher standard of living.

After a sumptuous vegetarian meal specially prepared for me, I wondered how many Mangals, in how many different places, are spending their days in the name of Gandhi. Anyway, not only in Osaka or Nagoya, Indian restaurants are doing well all over Japan, just as Chinese in our country. At a meeting at the Indian Embassy, the deputy ambassador, Biren Nanda told me that there were over 400 Indian restaurants in Tokyo.

Japanese are Indophiles. Many Japanese have learnt the Indian way of cooking, eventually opening restaurants and making a living out of it. But a visit to the *Ganga* restaurant under the Tokyo Opera Tower pricked my heart when I saw that this restaurant with the name of the holy Ganga served not only alcohol and meat abundantly, but also beef with *naan*[9] .

[24 March, 2002]

[8] Food cooked in an earthen oven / a method of Indian cooking
[9] A kind of bread

# Only One Room Less

Japan's capital, Tokyo is only three hundred and eighty years old. This city, then known as Edo had no infrastructure before that. Gradually, the political activities of Japan shifted from Kyoto to Tokyo with the Royal family shifting base to the Imperial Palace in Tokyo and subsequently, Tokyo became the centre of trade and economic activities. The region surrounding Tokyo was popular for farming but now besides farming, industrial units of coal, steel and other products are set up there. After the Second World War, ninety three percent of Japan's production capacity was destroyed and even today, Japan is a pauper in natural resources. Till 1868, Nagasaki, the main port of Japan, had permission to trade with only two countries – China and Holland.

Tokyo is considered to be the world's most expensive city. In fact, it cost me about fifteen thousand bucks from the airport to the Sheraton Hotel by taxi. After 1991, people started realizing that they were paying two hundred dollars for things that could be bought for a mere sixty dollars in other countries. Even the goods produced in Japan were cheaper in other countries than in Japan itself. I was extremely surprised to find coffee priced at three hundred and sixty yen outside the Sheraton coffee house. On my first visit to Japan, in the same café I had paid four hundred yen for a coffee. Next day, Japan's most prominent economist, Professor Sumimura of Shiga University had told me that the country has been trying to reduce prices for the last five to six years.

Land is extremely scarce in this country. Even in luxurious five star hotels, the rooms are small on an average. Osaka's Kansai airport is built on water and it is said that the airport will only last for few more years before completely sinking into the ocean. With one hundred and twenty million people and eighty two million vehicles, the people prefer travelling by train. In Tokyo, on an average a person spends around four hours commuting to and from work. There is a strange situation on tube stations here. Strong men, called marshals, are deputed at the gates of the compartments during peak hours to push people into the trains that have come filled from the previous stations. One can never think of carrying even a briefcase during the office hours.

In Tokyo, you do not find New York's long line of splendid cars, or fashionable young ladies like in Paris. Tokyo is engulfed in a strange kind of sadness and quietness. Tokyo has the Imperial Palace and the Tokyo Tower; each tree and plant by the roadsides in Tokyo is pruned and well maintained; but still life here does not seem to be vibrant, it seems suffocating. While strolling along the beautiful lake in front of the Imperial Palace, I recalled an Urdu verse of Javed Akhtar:

*Sabse khushi ka faasla bas ek kadam hai,*

*Har ghar mai bas ek hi kamra kam hai.*[10]

[31 March, 2002]

[10] Everyone is just a step away from happiness; every house is short of just one room.

# If There is Heaven on Earth…

The German poet, Goethe referred to Switzerland as a vast and extremely glorious country. The cities of Switzerland are clean and beautiful. The centre of attraction for people from across the world is its natural and unparalleled beauty. Switzerland, bordered by Germany, France and Italy, is a multi-lingual country with German, French and Italian being the widely spoken languages in the border areas. Besides these three languages, Romansh is spoken in the central part of Switzerland.

The citizens of Switzerland are directly involved in the law-making process. Besides elected representatives, if any citizen, a body of citizens or the citizens of a particular region can get one hundred thousand signatures establishing a constitutional amendment, it becomes a law. In India too, such proposals are given but the Parliament is not obliged to make them laws.

Mountains comprise sixty percent of the country's total area. The whole area being replete with mountains and rivers, hydroelectricity is available in abundance. Glaciers cover about two thousand square kilometres with the Rhine and the Rhone being the two major rivers. These rivers have the same significance for Switzerland as the Ganga and the Yamuna have in India. Unemployment is not a problem and tourism having been developed as an industry is a strong pillar of the economy here.

Switzerland's total population of approximately ten million is equal to that of Kolkata. After the Second World War, people from all over started migrating there. There is nothing special about the literature, art and culture of this country but its scenic and picturesque landscapes have attracted writers and artists from across the globe. Voltaire, Byron, Wordsworth among many others adopted this country as their own. Rousseau's essays caused a great stir in this country once. Shooting of films is quite common here. Thousands of indigenous and foreign films have been shot here.

According to the constitution of Switzerland, the President and Vice-Presidents are elected alternatively every year. The main objective of this is not to let one individual have complete supremacy. Except for these two posts, elections for all other posts are held every four years. This country has been neutral in international conflicts for many years. In spite of that, it is obligatory for every citizen to serve in the military.

Though Switzerland has not accepted the membership of the NATO or the United Nations, it acts as an observer nation at the UN. That is to say, the country pays money to the United Nations but cannot cast a vote. This country is not a member of the European Economic Union either.

The banks of this country are famous all over the world for their secret accounts. Delicious chocolates, expensive watches and the beautiful country mesmerize everyone. The country has been known by various names over the years - Schweiz, Svizzera, Svizra and now Switzerland. Wonderfully developed, well organized, clean and safe, all these attributes have given Switzerland the distinction of being called "Heaven on Earth".

[7 April 2002]

# International City – Geneva

During the two World Wars, when Europe was almost ruined, Switzerland was still safe. Hence when the other European nations were engaged in re-building, Switzerland made itself strong from the point of view of economy and trade. Geneva has become the Mecca for the meetings of international organizations. The World Health Organization, the Red Cross, the International Labour Organization and a number of other government and non-government organizations have set up their headquarters in this city. Seminars, conferences, lectures and exhibitions are held round the year. Every conference hall is well furnished with all modern amenities, including translation facilities of all the major languages of the world.

The first time I went to Geneva, it was the third week of June. Since the captain announced, that we would soon be landing in Geneva, I had been trying to look down through the window but I could not see anything except white clouds. On de-boarding, I realized that it was raining silently! It did not have a shrill, jarring sound like the rain in Kolkata or Mumbai. In June, the sun rises here at about three in the morning and sets at nine in the evening; that is to say, days are longer and nights, shorter. Geneva, located on western border of Switzerland, has France on its west and Italy, to the south. Since it borders France, most people speak French. The city is famous for Lake Geneva as it is situated on the banks of the lake. The river Rhone also crosses this city. There are a number of magnificent buildings on the banks of the river. The hundred and forty feet high Jet d'Eau fountain at the southern bank of the river is the prime centre of attraction for the tourists during summer.

Though Geneva is a small city, it is extremely beautiful. It is Switzerland's third largest city. Local people call Geneva by different names - Genève, Genf, Ginevra. It is a city where people from all over the world come to find a solution to their differences and conflicts. According to an estimate, one third of Geneva's population is made up of foreigners. One of the reasons for that is that the headquarters of many international organizations are set up here. Continual discussions on a number of subjects, issues and conflicts echo in the buildings of Geneva day and night.

The biggest advantage of being in Geneva is that one can travel to nearby countries very conveniently. Rome is a few hours' ride by train and so is Frankfurt. Cleanliness is given great importance in this city. It is a crime to throw garbage on roads or in public places. Generally, Switzerland is a law-abiding nation. The culture, civilization and society of this country are perhaps more developed than ours in many respects. We need to learn amiability, gentility, humility and discipline from them. Sparkling clean, with neither lies nor theft, everything is well-organized, every tree and plant well groomed, every road swept clean, plenty of hotels and conference halls and a wonderful ambience, all these factors make Switzerland's much sought after city Geneva, an international city.

[14 April 2002]

# Revolving Wheel of Time

The first time I went to Zurich, it had drizzled in the morning and the weather was very pleasant. The moment I came out of Zurich station, a cold breeze filled my mind and body with freshness and enthusiasm. I saw a bridge on crossing the wide road and unconsciously moved towards the bridge and went across. There, on both sides of the road were showrooms of the world's most renowned companies – Bally, Cartier, Prada, Christian Dior, Boss - you name it and it was there. While I was wandering around window-shopping, quickly calculating the value in Swiss francs of the money I had on me, I saw a lane next to a big shop of spectacles. In the middle of this lane I saw a Rolex showroom. Even before going for any foreign trip, the one thing that was always at the top of my shopping list was a Rolex watch. I had already calculated the cost of my favourite model of Rolex from an in-flight catalogue on my way to Zurich.

On both the sides of the lane, were large shops of watches and jewellery with smaller shops selling Swiss chocolates in the middle. I entered through the big glass door of the Rolex store and handed the slip carrying the details of the Rolex I wanted, to the Swiss salesgirl. A well-dressed Indian entered the shop. I smiled on seeing him. He extended his hand to greet me and introduced himself as Manu Chhabria. His name was familiar somehow, but we had not met before. I shook his hand with warmth. He asked, "Have you come here for the first time?" When I nodded, he said, "You can get a discount of thirty to thirty five percent in here." Manu spoke in Hindi so that the Swiss salesgirl would not understand.

I said that as it was a company showroom, I was hesitant to ask even for five percent discount. He talked to the manager and got me the watch at a discount of thirty percent. After that I explained how to get a discount at authorized company showrooms to many of my friends. Now I calculate the cost of watches after deducting twenty five percent of the written price in foreign countries.

After almost three years, when I happened to meet Manu Chhabria at London's Heathrow airport, the first question he asked on recognizing me was, "Are you looking for a watch here too?"

Manu Chhabria, who lived life in his own style, is no more. No one could think of the death of the wealthy Chhabria, who lived life wonderfully and with zeal. I was sad that the person, who had helped me get a watch at a discount, could neither get any relief in God's watch nor could he figure out the wheel of time. Moving with this wheel of time, my memories and I headed off to another city and another incident.

[21 April 2002]

# What Should I Call Our Culture?

It is said that every country has its own culture, to which its history and tradition make important contributions. If you understand what culture is, then you have to agree that it is difficult, if not altogether impossible, to define it. It is the amalgamation of varied views that contributes to the development of the culture of a society. The continuous debate ensures rejection of the more obsolete parameters with the inclusion of newer progressive ones. The knowledge of right and wrong with the standardization of values in the context of the members of society is essential. Every culture selects its own friends and foes both from within and outside its boundaries.

Travelling around the world, I realized that culture is like music in the sense that neither can be separated on the basis of countries and castes. Culture is not permanent; it is continuously evolving. Every culture silently imbibes qualities of another culture. The West has been as influenced by our culture as we have been by theirs. It has been a symbiotic relationship. There is much more vegetable intake in the West now and a lot of them have turned vegetarians inspired by Jain preachers. If our culture has given them the concept of non-violence, we have learnt perseverance, discipline and sanitation from them.

While wandering on the roads of Britain, some sights felt so familiar and some faces, so known, it was as if I was on the roads of Mumbai or Kolkata. The hilly areas of Switzerland reminded me of Kashmir. The Heaven on Earth reminded of the Heaven of Hindustan. But this remembrance came with the knowledge of all the destruction and it pained me to see that on the one hand, the Swiss had preserved their heaven, while on the other hand, we had successfully destroyed ours. It was there that I understood that it was man who created culture, tradition, myth and fantasy, and it was man who finally destroyed them. That was the only reality of this world.

My extravagant lifestyle in those years and wanderlust ('vagabond' in their words), had led my family members to believe that I had gone astray. They felt that all this was not appropriate in "our" culture. While boating on Lake Geneva, thinking about these issues, I would be reminded of Pablo Neruda's lines:

*Main karoonga koshish samajhne ki*
*Kya karna chahiye kya nahin*
*Isi tarah to thehra sakta hoon nyaysangat*
*Un raaston ko jin par bhatak sakta hoon main....* [11]

The pleasant weather of Switzerland took me from Geneva to Luzern, Luzern to Zurich, Zurich to Interlaken and Interlaken to Jungfrau. I kept thinking about how Switzerland could remain absolutely unaffected and neutral during the World War II? It had neither friends nor foes. It supported neither Germany nor England. It has kept everyone's money, from a Jew to a Nazi. It has stood by its claim of being neutral by supporting no one.

[28 April, 2002]

[11]...I will try to understand,
what should be done or not done,
only this way, I can justify
the ways on which I can wander...

# Our Culture and Theirs

The concept of society and morality has plunged down as never before. There is a huge gap between the speech and actions of most people. We need to take account of our misgivings and faults, evaluate them and work towards changing the system. The problem is that there is no one who can hold a mirror to society and point out that this is where we are going wrong. The West accepts its changing social mores and circumstances with complete transparency. There is no place for deceits, show off or pretence in the social structure. How can we compare ourselves to the West when we are unwilling to bring any changes to our society and insist on hiding behind the veil of religion and culture?

Travelling by train from Zurich to Interlaken, I was trying to absorb the extraordinary beauty outside. On the seat in front of me was a newlywed Pakistani couple on their honeymoon. I had just struck up a conversation with them, when the train microphone came alive announcing my name, requesting me to see the person in charge of the compartment. Confused and praying lest something unfortunate should happen, I stood up. Leaving my things with the couple, I moved towards the head of the compartment. As soon as I showed the man my passport, he passed me an envelope and told me that I had paid extra at the ticket window by mistake. When I opened the envelope, I found twenty eight Swiss francs in it. I was surprised that all this effort was put in just to return a few hundred rupees, which I had paid extra due to miscalculation of the exchange rate. That is how truthful and honest Switzerland is! Neat, clean and beautiful! The greenery is refreshing for the eyes and the lakes relax the heart. With no filth in the lake and the water as clean as a mirror, cruising on the lakes on the two sides of Interlaken has its own pleasure.

There is a small hotel by the name of Eden Nova right in front of the Interlaken station where I stayed during my first visit. On the other side of the hotel is a port, from where one can board a ship to cruise the lake. At that time, I was using a Euro Rail travel pass which enables the holder to travel to all the seventeen European countries by train, bus or waterways as many times as they want within the validity period. To utilize this, I would take a cruise on the lake every morning and enjoy the scenic views of green hillocks dotted with toy-like houses amid strong winds.

While facing the strong winds on the ship's deck, I would often wonder why our country could not be disciplined. We have inherited civilization and culture. But simply singing paeans of our inheritance does not serve any purpose. Our society has become very weak and helpless. Where will this culture and perspective take us?

[5 May, 2002]

# Other Shore of the Indian Ocean

I had gone to attend an eight-day youth workshop in Durban, South Africa. It was a good opportunity to get to know the working of the United Nations Organization. Besides, it was the only continent I had not yet visited. The Father of our Nation, Mahatma Gandhi is as well known in South Africa as he is in India. It is said that Mohandas Karamchand Gandhi became "Gandhi" in South Africa. It was there that he left his legal practice and chose the path of fighting for the rights of people that led him to become such an integral part of our own freedom struggle. Gandhi, who lived by the mantra of non-violence, got his inspiration in South Africa. His time in South Africa has been explored in great detail in the *Collected Works of Mahatma Gandhi*. Even today, about six hundred kilometres from Durban, a huge, well-organized ashram is being run in his name.

Every third person in Durban is of Indian origin. While walking on the streets, you feel as if you are in an Indian city among African and Caucasian tourists. At times in the whole crowd, you would hardly see a couple of non-Indians. I found it fitting that it was Durban that served as the other shore of the Indian Ocean.

Many Indian families have settled in this other country of Gandhi, migrating there over a hundred years ago. They are Indian by appearance, with deities in their homes, women wearing *saris*[12], putting *sindur*[13] in the parting of their hair, dancing to the tunes of Hindi film songs and the youth berating the corruption and mismanagement in India; and yet these people cannot speak a word of Hindi. Speaking African languages fluently, most of these people have never been to India and do not know anything about their native place.

During my twelve-day stay in South Africa, I met a number of young people of Indian origin who dreamt of visiting India at least once. But it pained me to see that these Indians, who had settled so far away from home, did not call themselves Indians; they called themselves South Africans. When I met Ila Gandhi, I felt very happy that Gandhi's granddaughter was a Member of Parliament there. But my happiness was short-lived until I heard her declare, "I am not an Indian! I am a South African and I will remain so!" Almost all of the Indians settled here have the same attitude. They criticize corruption while making fun of India's governance system. They are, in fact, hesitant to link themselves to India in any way.

South Africa needs Gandhi's precept of non-violence even today. Incidents of robbery and violence are increasing by the day in the capital city of Johannesburg. The situation has worsened so much that entire sections of population have migrated from one region to another. But whatever be the situation, at least Gandhi is still revered there. Gandhi's other nation may have forgotten his message but he still lived in their hearts.

[12 May, 2002]

[12] 6 or 9-yard long cloth wrapped round the waist in different styles- worn by Indian women

[13] Vermilion powder put in the parting of the hair by Hindu married women

# May God Give Everyone Sagacity

While living in South Africa among the Indians and their children, who were either brought to South Africa in the 19th century or had immigrated later with a desire to prosper, Gandhi had seen a dream of struggle and self-sacrifice. He understood the value of his life among them. During my sojourn in South Africa, I remembered Gandhi many times. There is no doubt that Gandhi is the icon of our struggle for independence, but Mohandas is much closer to the sensitivities and experiences of an ordinary man.

Being aware of one's weakness is a sign of greatness. I had the opportunity of getting to know Gandhi as Mohandas while visiting the many places in Durban, Pietersburg and Johannesburg. Most of them touched my heart but I was extremely sad on seeing Phoenix. Only a platform is left of Gandhi's house. Everything was in ruins. People say that underworld activities are carried out there now but the government is not doing anything about it. While establishing the settlement, Gandhi had named it Phoenix because a phoenix never dies; it rises from its ashes to be resurrected. It hurt me to see Phoenix reduced to ashes with no hope of resurrection.

But why blame only South Africa? Has our own country cared for Gandhi? For Gandhi, Hindus and Muslims were like his two eyes and it is shameful that there is so much hatred between them in the name of religion. One cannot truly understand Gandhi's struggle without seeing South Africa. At times I wonder if Gandhi should have gone back to South Africa after India's independence. Perhaps then he would have become the father of the world. Staying here, all he got was death at the hands of Nathuram Godse.In the Royal Hotel in Durban, an Indian had asked me in his broken Hindi, "Why was violence being perpetuated in India, where Gandhi was born, where he had given the precept of non-violence?"

Gandhi knew that every individual regardless of his skin colour, his clothing, his country or religion, is ultimately a human being. He will have to learn how to coexist; he will have to learn tolerance of other people and their religions.

[19 May 2002]

# Treaty Does Not Give Security to Insecure Public

Marcel Proust writes, "None of us had time to live life's real dramas that luck had written for us. That only makes us old – only that, nothing else. Wrinkles and creases on our faces indicate to those passions, addictions and insights that had come to meet us, but we were not at home." I find this quote very relevant when I think of why we could not adopt Gandhi's philosophy in our lives.

The moment my eyes opened, shaking off the Gandhian thoughts, I realized that the South African Airways plane I was on was about to land in Johannesburg. Until a few decades ago, an African or an Asian needed a permit to even move around in the 'White only' areas. The only people with these permits were those who worked in the households of the Caucasians, doing menial chores.

It is true that treaties do not necessarily give security to an insecure public. In spite of so many documents, treaties and changes in the law, the Africans are yet to receive total relief. Nelson Mandela devoted his entire life to the upliftment of Africa and its people but the bitter truth is that even today Africans are looked down upon in many parts of the world.

During those years in Johannesburg, this insecurity had led to extreme violence towards non-Africans. It was dangerous to be found on the streets even at seven in the evening. Every NRI that I met in Johannesburg told me not to leave the hotel in the evening in any condition. I was advised to avoid the main parts of the city even during daytime and to never stop my car at a red light. When I had called my friend Rohit Khandelwal to book a hotel room in Johannesburg for me, he told me very bluntly that no way should I make the mistake of staying at a hotel in the city. He made arrangements for my stay in the outskirts of the city and told me not to take a taxi from the airport as most of them were kidnappers. I was told to use the shuttle instead. I had dismissed his concerns with a smile, but on reaching Johannesburg I realized that the whole city was living in the shadow of terror. There was danger everywhere. Entire banks, offices, houses had shifted locations and there was row after row of huge, vacant buildings lining the roads of Johannesburg.

I could not understand the reason for all this violence. I couldn't fathom the fear and terror the people of this beautiful city lived in. The only conclusion I ever arrived at was that maybe this was all a result of the extreme cruelties they had been subjected to in the colonial times.

[26 May, 2002]

# City of Our Countrymen – Durban

Acharya Kalyanmal Lodha, one of the best Hindi scholars amongst the people I know always said to me, "Sundeep, you write well. Just write with a little imagination." "How do I write with imagination?" I asked. Lodha*ji* said, "At least try!" I could not understand how to write by imagining something. Everything was just so different from my imagination. When I came to know about the workshop in Durban, my imagination was very different.

The moment I landed at Durban airport, I realized that this city was also different from my imagination. It is said that one should dream and only then do dreams become reality. Durban airport was smaller than what I had expected but what surprised me most was that everyone at the airport: the employees of South African Airways, the customs officer, the porters, the immigration officer and even the person standing outside with the board "Welcome to Durban UN Conference" –were all of Indian origin. Only the bus driver was of African origin. I knew that I would see Indian faces in Durban but I had not expected so many of them. I shook hands with the boy carrying the board and introduced myself. He shook my hand and pointed me to the bus. Boarding the bus, I exchanged smiles with the few people sitting inside and sat down. Once outside the airport, I saw a big hoarding with the words: "You are welcome to the conference city, Durban" with the sub-text, "We welcome the delegates coming to World Racism Conference". The whole city of Durban was buzzing with the conference. Foreign ministers, national leaders, intellectuals, thinkers, social workers from all over the world were going to participate in the three-day conference. Every hotel, every meeting hall, every vehicle in the city had been booked by the organizing committee.

The seminar on the prejudices of caste, colour and creed had been on the charts for two years. The whole city was enthusiastic as if the guests were visiting everyone personally. Our eight-day workshop was also organized as part of the racism seminar. One day before the seminar, a combined meeting of world's non-governmental organizations was held. In Hotel Holiday, youth representatives, who had come from different corners of the world, met to bring forward the point of view of the youth against racism. A separate meeting of the youth was also organized.

Arrangements for my stay were made in Coastland Apartments. It was a small apartment with a bedroom, combined drawing room and dining space and a bathroom. It was more organized and cleaner than my expectations. My roommate in the apartment was Cheema from Lesotho. In the room to the left was Miss Pavla Kurtosva from Czech Republic and to the right, Bob and Robert from Zimbabwe. I had to spend the next ten days with these people. Coastland Apartments had eight hundred such apartments, all of which were taken up by the various delegates visiting the conference.

A few blocks down the road from the apartment, to the left, were the shores of the Indian Ocean and to the right were hotels, pubs, restaurants and shopping centres. My apartment was on the 26th floor and looking out of my window at the Indian Ocean, I would feel a strange connect with this city which belonged to Indians outside India, and which was also situated on the shores of Indian Ocean like our own country.

[2 June, 2002]

# Who Can Forget the Struggle of Mohandas?

When Gandhi was known as Mohandas in Africa, all the Indian immigrants in the various colonies were called *coolies*. In India, *coolies* are hardworking people, who carry loads and were much more respected than in Africa. In Africa, every Indian was a *coolie* and was segregated from mainstream society. Just as in India, groups of untouchables lived in settlements outside the city. There was a fixed time within which they could enter the city. Terrible sanitary conditions prevailed in these settlements and the people were notorious. Mohandas made an association with these people and fought legal battles for them. To express his views, Mohandas had to rush to English newspapers. Though the newspapers honestly published whatever was sent to them, it did not reach the common educated Indians there. Mohandas felt the need of a newspaper in our language and founded the newspaper *Indian Opinion*. The first of its kind in Africa, it was published in Hindi, Tamil, English and Gujarati. Gandhi's thought of publishing a newspaper in these languages at that time, of not forgetting one's culture, of bringing people together through their language, thus making the community realize its worth, is commendable.

The hottest issue in the Durban Racism Conference was whether casteism was also a form of racism. A day before the racism seminar, I went to see the Crocodile Park which was a few kilometres outside Durban. The park housed crocodiles of all sizes and shapes. The park was so well organized that it was even possible to be photographed with a live cobra or python around one's neck. You could even jump on the back of a crocodile if you wanted.

In the inaugural session of the conference, Omar Farooq Abdullah, the then Minister of State for External Affairs, who was leading the Indian delegation, declared that India did not see casteism as a manifestation of racism. They were both separate issues and casteism should be kept out of this conference on racism. This led to a lot of protest amongst the masses with demonstrators outside the hall sporting t-shirts with the slogan – CASTEISM IS A PART OF RACISM.

Unfazed, Omar Farooq presented our country's views very succinctly and immediately, radio stations and TV channels, across the world echoed with the news that India considered the issues of casteism and racism separate. Omar Farooq brilliantly fielded all the remarks and questions from the countries that had thought of hemming India on the issue. Ghana's elderly Foreign Minister, who was sitting behind me, said with a smile, "This young minister of your country is very wise."

During the inaugural session, the hall was filled to capacity. I was tired of greeting people and shaking their hands. It made me very happy to see that people from all over the world had gathered there to discuss the problem of racism that day, finally supporting Gandhi, who had raised his voice against this issue all alone decades ago.

[9 June, 2002]

# We Know Gandhi the Least

I had travelled all over the world before my trip to South Africa, but it was there that I felt I had finally come out of my cocoon. Though it was the same society and the same people, yet it was a very new world with thousands of my own countrymen. I realized how thrilling it was to see our cities, roads and society out of context. I saw a lot of things in South Africa – Cape Town with its toy story look, Johannesburg with the constant shadow of terror, the intoxicated Sun City and the humane Durban.

I met the foreign ministers, foreign secretaries, heads of non-government organizations and intellectuals from different corners of the world. I met the then Secretary General of the United Nations Organization, Kofi Annan and the then representative of non-government organization, Laria Visberg of Geneva there; and became quite friendly with Fredrik Daby, the then Chief Secretary of Global Compact Programme of the United Nations. I also met Ramgovind Mewa, who was a Member of Parliament and the ex-husband of Ila Gandhi. I spent a number of evenings with Mehul Patel, who was introduced to me by Pawan Agarwal of *Bhaskar* group. But the person who impressed me the most was Professor William Tiga Tita. He was one of the world's most prominent intellectuals and looked after Bill Gates' social trusts. I had never met such a wonderful orator. He could sway any opinion with just a few words.

After Durban, I met him again at a conference in New York. I told him that I was very impressed by him and wanted to spend some time with him. The same night he called me and came to my room for coffee. Extremely simple life, excellent style of speech, unusual style and completely new thoughts – such is Professor William Tiga Tita!

The workshop was being conducted at the Durban Royal Hotel. The arrangements for the stay of the various Heads of States and the many dignitaries had been done in a five-star hotel which was surrounded by security personnel. I had never seen such a huge gathering of national leaders. Many countries had even set up offices in the banquet hall of the hotel to ensure proper arrangements for their representatives.

During my visit, I heard about Hamid Seedat. He was a senior attorney in Durban and was an acknowledged scholar of the Gandhian history. He has a large personal library on Gandhi which houses journals and books published on Gandhi along with newspaper clippings from his various endeavours. A new building has also been constructed in place of the Durban jail, where Gandhi and Kasturba had lived. It was really only South Africa that knew everything about Gandhi. Though we Indians take pride in saying that we know Gandhi the best, it is us who know the least about him.

[16 June, 2002]

# Time of Death

Death is eternal. Death is an attribute of the body. Death is linked with birth. Death and life are the orders of the world. One who comes on this earth has to go; but when death is unnatural, not normal, one has to believe this truth mixed with a feeling of anger. The *Bhagwat Geeta* says, “Whatever happens is predetermined – everything, each and every moment, each and every time is predestined. Whatever has to happen, will happen.”

For Hindus nothing is greater than the truth that is written in the *Bhagwat Geeta*. I could not readily accept this truth in spite of being a Hindu. But in life I came across such incidents that I started believing in the *Geeta*, such as being saved from a snake bite in the forests of Africa and the sudden change in my plan of going to America's World Trade Centre on September 11, when it was attacked. But the incident that occurred last week made me believe absolutely that no one can evade providence, howsoever bitter or cruel it may be. Whatever has to happen is predetermined, is immutable and is irrevocable. During my foreign trips, many incidents happened that gave me goosebumps but I can perhaps never forget one incident. Particularly, the face of driver Ramratan, who I could not save, haunts me many times in my sleep.

On Saturday, 8th June when I came out of the bungalow of Nalini Florist situated at Victoria Terrace near Camac Street, I saw Jhumarmal*ji* Bacchawat. After wishing me, he said, “Well, you are coming for tomorrow's programme, aren't you?” I answered, “Yes, I received a phone call from Daga*ji* but Kolaghat is a little far.” He immediately responded, “Do come; at least get a photograph taken with me.” I reminded him that last month he was photographed with me in a get-together organized by Chhatarsingh*ji* in Horticulture Garden. He laughed, "People are right when they say that you are expert in everything. You keep an account even of photographs."

The next day at 7:45 AM, I reached Kankaria Park. We had to go to Kolaghat, where Bacchawat*ji* was going to donate a hundred thousand rupees to a rural organization. Sardarmal*ji* Kankaria, Tilokchand*ji* Daga, Sampatmal*ji* Bacchawat, Surender*ji* Banthia etc. were already at the residence of Harakchand*ji* Kankaria when I reached.

Around 8:10 AM, Jhumarmal*ji* came and said he had been delayed, waiting for Sardarmal*ji* at breakfast. While requesting us to hurry up, Sardarmal*ji* suggested taking two cars instead of three. After a little friendly bickering, it was decided to go by three cars.

After picking up Abhaysingh*ji* Surana from Mangoe Lane, Bacchawatji's blue Hyundai was in front, with Sardarmal*ji* in the front and Bacchawat*ji* and Tilokchand*ji* Daga at the back. Next was my white Cielo, in which Jhumarmal*ji*'s brother, Sampat*ji* Bacchawat accompanied me and the last was a rust Tata Safari, in which Abaysingh*ji* Surana travelled with a few other people.

About ten kilometres before reaching Kolaghat, we stopped at the bidding of Bacchawat*ji*. As soon as the cars stopped, refreshments started and after about ten minutes, we started again in the same order –first Hyundai, then Cielo and then Tata Safari.

The office-bearers of the organization were to meet us at a famous dhaba of Sardar*ji* at Kolaghat.

At the dhaba, everyone thought of ordering lassi instead of tea or coffee. I refused to have any as I did not feel like it and I was not satisfied with the cleanliness. But Harakchand*ji* Kankaria forcibly handed me a glass.

We came to the cars after finishing the lassi, when Abhaysingh*ji* Surana said that he wanted to sit with Jhumarmal*ji*. Sardarmal*ji* was fine with it and he went towards the Tata Safari. As a result of this exchange, in the back seat of the blue Hyundai were Sardarmal*ji* with Bacchawat*ji* and in the front Tilokchand*ji* Daga. Since Sardarmal*ji* was in the Tata Safari, it was now in the front and at the rear end was the blue Hyundai. My Cielo remained in the middle.

The office bearers were in a Tata Sumo ahead of the Safari. While getting into the car, I said to Sampat*ji*, "It is 10:20 AM. We will reach about an hour late." At that time, the driver of Bacchawat*ji* blew the horn loudly. I pointed out that their driver was driving very fast, which was not good. My driver Bhadro said, "Sir, I had also told him at dhaba that he should not overtake like that on the highway." I told my driver that he did not have to follow him but should drive carefully and slowly. Sampatmal*ji* agreed with me. Suddenly we heard a crash and my driver shouted, "Sir! Oh God, what has happened! They won't survive. It was such a fatal collision."

I turned around and saw the blue Hyundai come to a halt by the side of the road after spinning around twice. It had collided with a trailer carrying iron. Having taken stock of the situation, I shook my driver and asked him to be careful and stop the car. Sampatmal*ji* was bewildered till then and asked, "What has happened?"

Responding to him, I said, "It is an accident…." I rushed towards the car. My driver reached there before me. He was a nervous wreck and was shouting. I shook him hard and said, "Control yourself. We have to save these people."

The door on Bacchawat*ji's* side was fully open. I held his hand and tried to pull him out of the car but his body was stuck. My driver pulled him by his feet and we laid him on the road. I felt for his pulse but could not find any.

I put my ear to his chest and pumped it but when I looked at his face, I saw his nose had bled soaking his body with blood. I took a long breath and got up. By then Sardarmal*ji* and Surender*ji* Banthia had reached us. I told Banthia*ji* that Bacchawat*ji* was not responding.

People from the area had also gathered. They pulled the driver out and I tried to help Abhaysingh*ji*. He moaned when we sprinkled water on his face. A flap of flesh from his forehead, right above his eye, was hanging loose. I closed my eyes and when I put it back in place pressing it with my hand; he cried out and almost lost consciousness.

He was moved into the Tata Sumo and they drove off quickly, saying that they were taking him to Tamluk Hospital and we should also get there.

Daga*ji* was also pulled out with the help of people. His foot had been caught in the car. His face was red with blood and he was groaning. We laid Daga*ji* in the Tata Safari and Sardarmal*ji* took him to the hospital. After that I asked Harakchand*ji* to sit in the front of my Cielo and laid the driver at the backseat and sat along with him. I asked my driver to quickly start the car. The driver Ramratan was fully conscious. He was crying out with pain and his body was soaked with blood. The seat of the car had turned red with blood.

At Tamluk Hospital, we saw the Sumo and Abaysingh*ji* was being taken away. It was a small one room nursing home. At the same moment, Surender*ji* Banthia and Sampat*ji* carrying Jhumarmal*ji* in an ambulance reached there. I told the doctor, "I think that the person outside is dead but if you agree, do not tell his brother." He checked Jhumarmal*ji* in the ambulance and nodded to me. I informed Surender*ji* and Harakchand*ji* about it in private. After giving first-aid to the driver, we put him in the ambulance as well.

We had decided to take everyone to Kolkata after first-aid but it was also essential to make arrangements for safe journey to Kolkata. There was the question of providing oxygen to the driver. The hospital authorities were dilly-dallying in giving oxygen but after much hullabaloo by some neighbourhood boys I had asked for help, oxygen cylinders were taken out.

When I had gone to the boys, I had called Kolkata from an STD booth to inform the office and asked people there to make required arrangements at the Jain Hospital, Howrah. Abaysingh*ji's* head injury was still bleeding and it could endanger his eye. The doctor said that he would have to put stitches but he did not have enough anaesthesia.

There was no time to think. When I agreed, he said, "Give it to me in writing or give me any document as your identity proof."

I do not know why but I always keep my passport in my bag. I had just taken the passport out when the crowd shouted and forced the doctor to put in the stitches without any formalities. I took Abhaysingh*ji*'s hand in my hand. I held his feet and another person, his other hand. Perhaps the injection had worked. He kept on moaning and the doctor kept on stitching his wound. My eyes were also closing. I came out and sat down, leaning against a wall. Perhaps I felt giddy in that environment of fear, tension, heat, anxiety and blood. After a few minutes when I opened my eyes, I found myself lying down on the back seat of my car. The A.C. was on and people were standing around the car. I got up immediately and rushed towards the hospital. Stitches had been put on Abhaysingh*ji*'s wound. Daga*ji* was out of danger and he was also being sent to Jain Hospital by an ambulance. I went to Harakchand*ji* and after asking him to sit in the car, requested for one more ambulance. After about fifteen minutes, another ambulance came. After laying Surana*ji* in it, I and Harakchand*ji* started for Kolkata.

After half an hour, as soon as my mobile phone came in the range of network, I started getting calls one after the other. Everyone had only one question, "What happened?" What could I say? I was tired of speaking. My head was already heavy.

My phone did not stop ringing. I knew that with my phone call, the news would spread like wildfire but I had not realized that it would spread so fast. On reaching the hospital, when my attention diverted from the crowd of people and turned to my clothes, I found that my *pyjama* was soaked with blood. I had washed my face, forehead and hands before starting from the hospital. So much blood had never touched my body before. Not only that - even my chest under the clothes was drenched with blood.

After reaching the hospital when I asked about the driver, I came to know that he had died on the way. Neither my laying him in the car to take him away hastily was fruitful nor the oxygen. The doctor failed and

I also failed. The driver Ramratan was in much better condition than all the others but perhaps Lord Ram did not want to save this Ratan because his end had come. I was stunned to hear that Ramratan had died on the way. Perhaps that is why the *Geeta* seems tot be right that whatever has to happen, will happen. No one can change it.

Time for the death of Jhumarmal*ji* Bacchawat was fixed between 10:25 AM and 10:30 AM. His end had to come at that time. If only Bacchawat*ji* had come to the Kankaria house on time, all this could have been avoided. If we had taken two instead of three cars, perhaps then also this moment would have passed. But the time (of death) had to come and at its determined time. It came, finished its job and passed away.

Jhumarmal*ji*'s death was not only the loss to the Bacchawat family but also to the entire Jain community. The community will always feel the absence of such a personality. Jhumarmal*ji* is no more but he will always be remembered as a prominent member of the community. The walls of South Kolkata Terapanthi building will always remember him. His absence will always be felt in the meetings of friends. Every patient visiting Churu hospital will bless him and the Terapanthi community will never be able to forget his work. My homage to omnipresent Jhumarmal*ji*!

Two other things associated with this incident that I would never be able to forget – firstly, I have no hesitation in writing that the help people in that rural area provided us was so much more than what their urban counterparts would have in the time of need; and secondly, the inhuman behaviour of the photographer Ashish, who had accompanied us. He was riding on the backseat of Safari. After seeing the accident, he neither stopped to offer his help, nor did he call anyone else informing them. Perhaps that is the way of the world and such is the time of death.

[23 June, 2002]

# The Wealthiest Nation

Europe is unparalleled in terms of beauty and cleanliness. Amongst the many bigger and better known European countries is Luxembourg. Very small, almost the size of our Kolkata, Luxembourg is just less populated and economically very strong. Luxembourg has no capital, no provinces because the whole country is one city, one province and one nation. Japan is usually considered to be the richest nation in the world, but mathematically, Luxembourg ranks higher than Japan. The per capita income of Luxembourg is much more than that of Japan and sharing its borders with Belgium and Netherlands, this country is unique in itself.

In early 1996, I had applied for a visa to London but my passport was returned with a black rubber stamp by the British Deputy High Commission. My last stay in London had been very long, so my visa application was rejected on the grounds that I may settle there. I had not thought that it could happen and so had not gone for the visa myself. I had given the job to a travel agency. Stunned, I went from Ho-Chi-Minh Sarani to Chanakyapuri many times but the visa officials did not budge.

It was impossible for me to explain to them that I would not like to settle in London. I had no plans of living in a country where one has to even wash the dishes himself. I contacted everybody I could, tried every possible approach, but nothing worked. I was more anxious because once your visa is rejected by the British, the other European countries generally follow suit. That would mean that for the next five to seven years, the doors to Europe and America were closed to me and I put all my efforts into thinking of an excuse to visit any European country.

I had accepted that all efforts were in vain when Sitaram Sharma, who had been on various positions of several non-government organizations and had friendly relations with many ambassadors, talked to the British Deputy High Commission again on my behalf with no result. These foreigners did not trust my love for my country. One day, Sharma*ji* told me that a three-day conference was being held in Luxembourg on the occasion of the golden jubilee celebrations of the United Nations Organization and a seminar for the youth was also being organized. If I wanted, he could make an effort to register my name and get me an invitation. It was the first time I had heard of Luxembourg but it was the silver lining I was looking for. I thanked him profusely and agreed. But while leaving his office at the Tower House, I wondered that even if I got the invitation, who knew if I would get the visa or not, because Luxembourg did not have any High Commission or Embassy in India. So the visa would have to be granted by the High Commission of Belgium or Netherlands.

The invitation came and I had planned to go to the Belgium High Commission in Delhi in the morning, but then I received a fax that the seminar for the youth was cancelled. My hope for obtaining a European visa was completely over but Sharma*ji* got me registered as an observer for the conference. After a four-hour wait and one hour of questions during the interview at Belgium Embassy, I finally got the required permits to visit the world's richest nation – Luxembourg.

[30 June, 2002]

# Euro Rail Pass is a Blessing for Wanderers

It was drizzling when the airplane landed at the Zurich airport. Luxembourg was now just a train ride away. Some of the special trains on the Euro rail circuit such as Euro Star, Euro City etc. have facilities similar to five-star hotels in their first-class compartments. Foreign tourists to Europe can get a Euro rail pass which is valid for ten, fifteen, twenty-one, thirty or sixty days depending on the duration of their stay.

I travelled through Europe and Scandinavian countries using this pass of two-month validity when I first went to Europe. For people below twenty-six years of age this costs less. When I was travelling around Europe, I spent a number of nights in trains instead of hotels. I would always travel long distances so that it took at least seven to eight hours. I would take the night train, de-board in another city in the morning and finish my daily ablutions in the train itself. After getting off the train, I would put my luggage in the lockers available at the station, tour the city for the whole day and again take a night train to another city. Due to the Euro rail pass, not only travel was free, one could get a room-sized coach at a much lesser fare than charges at a hotel.

On reaching Luxembourg, I went straight to Hotel Sofitel. In the same hotel, other members of the Indian delegation, in which were ex-Cabinet Minister, Ramnivas Mirdha, the then speaker of Legislative Assembly of West Bengal, Hashim Abdul Halim, the then Minister of Parliamentary Affairs of West Bengal, Prabodhchandra Sinha, Sitaram Sharma, wife of ex-Central Minister Krishankumar and the then General Secretary of Indian Federation of United Nations Associations (IFUNA) Mrs. Usha Krishankumar and a representative from Kerala, were also staying.

Sofitel Hotel is divided into two parts, old and new. Usha Krishankumar and the representative from Kerala were in the old wing and the rest of us were in the new wing. Once in my room, I dialled Mirdha*ji*. I had been told that everyone except him had gone for the seminar. Just across a small bridge from Sofitel Hotel, there was a magnificent conference building of the European Union. The conference was to be held there. The conference had been inaugurated in the morning while I had reached in the evening, seven hours late via Switzerland as I had taken a train.

Though I was late, I felt relieved as there were no difficulties in obtaining the visa and crossing immigration. The decision to travel by train rather than by plane was also due to the fear of immigration officials. I was apprehensive that after seeing the black stamp of England, airport immigiration officials might send me back.

When I looked at the conference building from the window of my room in Sofitel Hotel, I was a little scared. It was the first time I was participating in such a conference and all the other members were scholars. I was just glad that the door to Europe was open for me, which I had lost all hope of. And I thought it was significant that I was sitting in a suite of the most luxurious five-star hotel of the world's richest nation, Luxembourg!

[7 July, 2002]

# The Country Whose President Goes to Market on a Bicycle

In Luxembourg, I had become quite friendly with some young European representatives; some of them are my good friends even today. After the conference, in the evening when we used to hang out, hearing them talk, I would be surprised. Some aspects of their life were a total revelation to me. There is a stark difference in their upbringing and ours. In European countries, everyone is expected to earn their own living by the age of sixteen; whereas in our country, mothers insist on feeding children with their own hands till the age of ten or twelve years.

There are very few Indians in Luxembourg. You could probably count them all on the fingers of your hand. There is no Indian Embassy or even a High Commission. There is only the Honorary Consul General. It was just our luck that a South Indian man was the receptionist in the older portion of Sofitel Hotel. Three-four days into the trip when we craved Indian food and our *paranthas* from home were all but finished, we were satiated by the *idlis*[14] he brought for us.

On the last day of the conference, the organizers had made arrangements to take us on a guided tour of Luxembourg. Through the day, I was increasingly surprised at everything I learned about that very small European nation. Luxembourg was not only the wealthiest nation of the world; it also had a wonderful social system. The government gave a monthly allowance equivalent to approximately eighty-five thousand Indian rupees to the unemployed along with various other subsidies. Ram Nivas Mirdha used to joke that if we settled there, we could enjoy ourselves while being unemployed for life! It is also obligatory for every student in Luxembourg to get military education. Another surprising fact is that, if you go to Luxembourg to learn their language, the government will give you a hefty scholarship besides meeting your boarding and lodging expenses as in Scandinavian countries,.

Standing outside the President's house, I was flabbergasted when the guide told us that the person, who had just come out - alone and on a bicycle - was the President. We could hardly believe him when he told us that while he is in office from nine to six, his entourage remains with him; but after that, he would go to the market on a bicycle to buy vegetables, the same as any ordinary man would. Amazing!

How can we ever hope to compare our country with Luxembourg? Their President goes around the city riding a bicycle, while in our country we have to face road blocks and traffic jams, to accommodate for just three hundred people engaging twelve thousand police personnel for security!

[14 July, 2002]

[14]A south Indian dish made by steaming the semi-liquid dough made from semolina

# Luxembourg

Luxembourg is neither famous for industry nor commerce; it does not have mines or oil-fields. Yet, Luxembourg is the wealthiest nation of the world. How? The main source of income for the country is its banks and insurance companies. The banks are so strict about their confidentiality, that people have more faith in banks here than in Switzerland. These banks are to Europe and America, what the Swiss banks are to India. The presence of multitude of banks and insurance companies and their simplistic rules, has led to the top firms of Europe establishing their headquarters in Luxembourg. While walking around in Luxembourg, it is not uncommon to find banks and insurance companies lined up on both sides of very wide roads.

The conference was being held just around the corner from our hotel, Sofitel. It was the time when the issue of a Schengen visa, which would be valid across the continent, was the hottest topic along with the use of common currency - Euro - throughout Europe. The fact that these issues would all be taken up, had the people and the delegates looking forward to the conference even more. When I reached the conference hall, I came to know that the conference had been cancelled. The Secretary General of the World Federation of United Nations Associations (WFUNA), Erskine Childers had breathed his last immediately after finishing his lecture during the inaugural session in the morning. The whole house was stunned. Even at the age of about sixty-eight years, Childers' contribution to the United Nations Associations was unmatched and there had been great expectations from him. After the sudden death of Childers, no one had felt like attending the seminar that day. But the show must go on and Haras Parera had been appointed as the interim General Secretary the next day and the conference had resumed.

I was introduced to many delegations that had come from different parts of the world. I also got an opportunity to work with Professor Aingner of Austria. For me it had been the first opportunity to meet so many scholars from across the world. There were twenty-three other youth representatives who were attending the conference as observers due to the cancellation of the youth conference. I was introduced to everyone in the evening at the pool-side bar of the hotel.

That had been my first interaction with the youth of Europe and I was surprised to know of their views, intellect, thought processes and lifestyle. There were no lies and no pretence; everything was transparent. When I offered a drink to a Yugoslavian girl who was studying in London, she very politely declined saying, "No, I don't want a drink because my pocket money does not allow it; I am here on scholarship." I was dumbstruck at the truthfulness of her response. If only the youth of our country adopted the progressive mindset instead of just the lifestyle of the West, perhaps we could become a better civilization.

[21 July, 2002]

# These Countries of Dreams

Europe has a number of small nations, even twelve or thirteen of which put together will be smaller than our country. Yet, each of these nations is so unique that one often wonders if it is a dreamland. One such country is Holland or The Netherlands where Van Gogh had painted his oh-so-famous sunflowers on a canvas. Holland is like an atom in the vast universe with colourful tulips adorning its fields, windmills rotating with the wind, the delicious aroma of fresh and hot produce from the multitude of bakeries, cows—fat and healthy, at the dairy farms producing rivers of milk and other products.

Looking at how the people of Holland treated their livestock made me question how could we ever say that we worship the cows in our country when we have not even been able to stop their killing? In Holland, the milk from the cows is directly let into tankers through a system of pipes. It is a crime to buy or sell unpasteurized milk there.

We have all heard about the Scotland Yard and the German police but it is the Netherlands that has the biggest drug cartel and the most famous red-light district in Eurasia. What is most amazing is that these things have been legalized in Holland for the pleasure of its many tourists. So instead of running from the law, they flourish with its blessing and contribute a great deal to the overall economy of the country. There are pre-organized bus tours from several spots in Holland to take the tourists around the city and introduce them to the country by night. They take you to areas where the great artist, Van Gogh, had once painted his own face on a canvas. Once again, Van Gogh's painting of sunflowers, which I had seen in a museum there, flashed before my eyes. I was also reminded of Irving Stone's *Lust for Life*, a wonderful novel written painstakingly on the life of Van Gogh.

It takes you back to the past with Van Gogh and his pain. His pain was so much that he finally cut his own ear off and was finally declared mad and demented by the society. Perhaps to be immortal, one has to be mad!

[28 July, 2002]

## Bicycle Riders are Specially Respected There

Even Britain and America are not as frugal as Holland. Jingling their gilder on the table, the Dutch say with pride, "This is gilder. Always stable." The markets of Holland decide the rates of even South African markets. Flowers are auctioned here. Philips, the most reliable name when it comes to electronics across the world is set up there. While it is true that Japan and Korea control most of the world's electronic market, but even they cannot hope to compete with the quality control of the Dutch. The flowers, cheese, milk and other dairy products of Holland are renowned. The Dutch factories for cutting and designing diamonds are major tourist attractions.

The main means of transportation for people are bicycles. People carry foldable bicycles with them and whenever they need it, they can just assemble it and pedal away. There are specialized lanes made in the middle of all major roads for bicycle riders. The Dutch law is more favourable to bicycle riders than any other. If there is a collision involving a bicycle and any other vehicle, then the driver of the motorized vehicle will be punished, regardless of whosoever maybe at fault. One of the more biased laws includes exemption from the traffic lights to the bicycle riders, even on major crossings!

It is believed that Holland is the "Crime capital" of Europe with most drug deals and murders are curated in the houseboats on the various canals running through its cities. More than twenty percent of the Dutch population live in houseboats anchored on these canals. It looks as if small boats are anchored on both sides of big drains and someone is living in a wooden room made on them!

One can witness the growth and prosperity of Holland from the moment one lands at Schiphol Airport in the capital city of Amsterdam. Schiphol Airport is among the top four busiest airports in the world. Along with big shopping centres, hotels, cinema halls and theatre, the magnificently large airport also boasts of a complete railway station within its premises. The trains plying between the city and the airport are much help to the tourists and locals alike.

The travel catalogues and information brochures on Europe often have a *Hawa Mahal*[15] like picture on it - of the legendary Central. This infamous building is Holland's Central Railway Station and most crowded area. There are plenty of hotels, cinema halls, shops, restaurants and coffee shops from all the countries of the world around this station. This area is also regarded as the "Crime Belt" of Europe. Around the Central Station, a fixed quantity of drugs is sold over the counter in the many coffee shops. It is normal to see tourists from different countries of the world sitting around chairs on the footpaths puffing away like nowhere else.

Throw in the red-light district and we have the most sought after destination in the world for youngsters and junkies. At times I wonder if there is some great pain beneath this free and unrestricted behaviour of the Dutch. It was a Dutch man who once said, "The louder a person laughs, deeper is his sorrow."

[4 August, 2002]

[15]A palace in Jaipur with a lots of windows, now a tourist spot

# Where a Woman's Body Is Sold Openly

The area around the Central Railway Station of Amsterdam city is like Mecca for the tourists. Just outside the station, there are rows and rows of hotels on both the sides of the road – Sheraton, Hilton, Holiday Inn, Four Seasons - you name it and it is there.

The first time I went to Holland, I knew a businessman Vijay Sikka who ran a three-star hotel, Albert Inn in the railway station area. I remember that I used to be afraid of travelling alone in the area because I had heard that all the Mafia kings of Europe visited there.

In between the hotels and coffee shops is the infamous red-light area. There are glass panes in the walls of these establishments with almost nude women sitting on stools, smoking; waiting for their next customer with their "rates" hanging on boards around their necks. You like what you see and are willing to pay the price for it, a shutter is dropped and you are pulled in to complete the transaction. It broke my heart to see women treated as a commodity up for sale!

The scene there was even more frightening than the red-light area of Mumbai as depicted by Hindi cinema. Even the red-light areas of Bangkok cannot compete with the Dutch and their window prostitution. This is the West, where everything is saleable. After all, it is Holland that is famous for the auction of flowers, where paintings are sold for up to multi-million dollars and it is this very nation that earned a lot of money by way of the slave trade.

How narrow minded is the West and yet they claim to give equal rights to women! I have heard that countries like Switzerland gave its women the right to vote just a couple of decades ago. We, on the contrary, are talking of giving thirty-three percent reservations to women in politics.

When I met an Indian friend after three years and asked him how his wife, Rosaria was, he responded saying that his wife was now Melina, not Rosaria. I was astounded at such a nonchalant reply. Whatever may be the ills of our society, whatever may be its anomalies, it still binds us together. It binds us to a system. It teaches us discipline and compels us to live in an ambience infused with social mores.

[11 August, 2002]

# Prabodh Babu Did Not Want to Tell That He Was a Minister

I had a chance of visiting Holland another time for business and for a third time while returning to Kolkata from a conference in Luxembourg. West Bengal's then Minister of Parliamentary Affairs, Prabodh Chandra Sinha was with me. He had insisted on returning to India after two days so that we could visit Holland together.

In Amsterdam, KLM Air services has its five-star hotel in the Central Railway Station area to cater to its Business Class passengers. Prabodh*babu* and I were taking advantage of this facility and staying there. On the opposite side of the road were a number of shops for tourists. Prabodh*babu* and I were strolling on the footpath but neither of us was in a particularly good mood. The conference and all the European food had tired us a bit. Prabodh*babu* had just said that he was missing home-cooked rice, when I happened to see a board with the inscription *Gandhi* and just below that, a picture of Gandhi, complete with his trademark glasses. We looked at each other and moved towards that board.

Our guess was absolutely correct. *Gandhi* was the name of a small, neat and clean Indian restaurant which could seat about ten people. Seeing two Indians walk into his establishment, the restaurant's owner-manager-waiter-cook rushed to greet us. Prabodh*babu* immediately blurted out, "Can you serve us rice and fish?" We occupied a table as soon as he nodded. The moment he went to the kitchen, Prabodh*babu* said, "Sundeep, don't tell him that I am a minister; it won't look nice." He had just finished saying that when this man returned. Placing water on the table, he asked Prabodh*babu*, "Where are you from?" On hearing his one word response, "Kolkata", he asked further, "Where is your office?" Unwittingly, Prabodh*babu* said, "Writer's Building." The man smiled and said, "Okay! So you have a job in a government office." We were very hungry but that man was more interested in talking. Perhaps, he had seen an Indian after many days.

When he came back with my bread-lentils and Prabodh*babu*'s fish-rice, looking at the high neck of Prabodh*babu*'s suit, he asked, "Only ministers wear these types of clothes in India. What do you do in a government office?"

Prabodh*babu* did not pay any attention to his comment and ordered another plate of rice and I could not stop laughing at the situation.

In foreign countries, whenever I have visited an Indian restaurant – whether it is *Gaylord* of London or *Taj* of Copenhagen, *Raj Mahal* of Tokyo or *Ganga* of South Africa – I am definitely reminded of this incident at the *Gandhi* restaurant of Amsterdam.

[18 August, 2002]

# Their Society and Ours

France – a country where you can see revolving markets, the biggest fashion centres of the world, beautiful night clubs, the Eiffel Tower and the sparkling River Seine in the twinkling lights of night. Most of the great painters of the world have lived there looking for their muses and the intellectuals have explored the city's streets. Before coming to France, and particularly Paris, my mother made me promise that I would stay away from night clubs. She was always anxious about me falling in love with a foreigner. My delaying of marriage added to this anxiety. In the past two years, there has never been a day when my mother had not raised the issue of my marriage during breakfast or dinner.

At the pizza corner of Charles de Gaulle Airport of France, I was talking to a lady and her son who told me that she had advised her son not to marry as he wanted to be a great painter. Being a painter required single mindedness and marriage destroyed this focus in her opinion. Whenever my mother tried to tempt me with a good offer of marriage, I was reminded of that lady at the pizza corner.

Not only to be a painter but to achieve greatness in any field, one needs to have complete dedication. Marriage may not destroy your dedication but it definitely disrupts it. I often think what if Lata Mangeshkar, Abdul Kalam, Ratan Tata and Atal Bihari Vajpayee had not persevered in their fields with dedication? Would they have achieved as much as they did if they had married?

I do not mean to imply that one cannot achieve anything after marriage. A person should just be honest about his relationships, his work and his goal to achieve them. Yet our society does not allow a person even the slightest honesty that my mother could just decline all the marriage offers saying I did not want to marry then; she always had to evade the issue by making excuses.

I often question the traditions, perspective and the mindset of our society. Fingers are pointed at those unmarried, their characters are assassinated and all sorts of allegations and judgments are passed on them. On the contrary, a married person, regardless of any vices, shortcomings or character flaws gets to live respectfully.

Pressure on the youth to get married in the Marwari society is perhaps more than in any other society of the world. It is in fact emotional blackmail. We boast of our Indian values and our traditional joint family system but the fact is that we, as a society are living under a cloak of these illusions. If we remove this cloak, we might also be able to bring forth personalities like Sartre, Albert Einstein, Charles de Gaulle, Nietzsche and Eisenhower.

[25 August, 2002]

# Afternoon at Montaigne

Avenue Montaigne is to Paris what Bond Street is to London or Fifth Avenue to New York or Connaught Place to Delhi. Not to forget, Park Street in Kolkata. There is no dearth of fashion and culture there. Be it Park Street or any other street in any corner of the city, there is always a small boutique, some small art gallery or people drinking tea or eating *samosas* in some shady corner. Rajiv Gandhi had once said, "Kolkata is a dying city." I beg to differ, for where else will you get the kind of life Kolkata has to offer? Kolkata is eternal. It will always be inhabited.

Getting back to Avenue Montaigne, it is not an ordinary street. It is the Mecca-Medina of fashion, where you have Gucci, Voyage, Hugo, Louis Vuitton and every other fashion label from across the world. Looking around, I was awestruck on seeing Hollywood actresses, singers and Parisians alike. Everyone dressed impeccably and impressively. It suddenly became clear to me why the driver had given me a look when I had asked for Montaigne.

One of the strangest things was that at the Louis Vuitton store, a buyer could only buy one item at a time. I could not understand the reason behind this restriction at such a huge store. Later on, I came to know that the Japanese went so mad after shopping at the Montaigne that they would buy all the things in the store and then sell counterfeit products.

When I came out of the store, a Chinese man at the corner of the square asked me in broken Hindi, "Do you want to buy something from Louis Vuitton? I can get you everything, though it will be a little costlier." When I asked him how, he said, "Every day girls go in there, buy one thing at a time and give them to us. We give them their commission and sell them to Japanese at a higher cost."

I then understood the whole strategy. First, use the original branded items, then copy them and fill the world's market with counterfeits. Montaigne is a greater example of the culture of fashion and consumerism than perhaps any other market of the world.

[1 September, 2002]

# France

Paris is synonymous with fashion. At little distance from the L'Oreal and Marne outlets, the Calvin Klein store carried clothes in shades of white only. Seeing such an abundance of clothing in my favourite colour automatically put the store at the top of my list.

Exactly opposite to the Calvin Klein store are the stores of Joel Mender and Barbara Bui. There one could find doll-like Japanese girls coming out of the stores, happy with their shopping. There was a large crowd of people all around and for these people happiness was then and there. But my happiness had to wait until the next day when I would visit the art galleries and museums of Paris.

As I stood looking at the Chanel and Christian Dior stores, an elderly lady said, "Have you come to see its glory? Once there used to be only classic and extraordinary things here. Now all sorts of dresses are sold here in the name of fashion! Women today have completely changed." When I asked, "Aunty, what happened to the earlier ones?" she responded, "What is this "aunty"? My name is Liza Barky. I used to be a model. Everything has changed with the freedom given to women. The complete look of Chanel has changed". Not just Paris, the whole country of France is famous for being fashion conscious, so much so, that even people sunbathing on beaches of Nice or gambling in casinos at Monte Carlo are fashionably dressed.

Travelling by car from Nice to Monte Carlo was much more fun than even travelling on the glossy roads of Switzerland. I also developed a taste for Lebanese food while travelling through Nice and Monte Carlo – a necessity then but I did acquire the taste eventually. At that time, Indian food was not readily available and I had neither knowledge nor the taste for Chinese or Mexican vegetarian food.

Eating Chinese hard rice for two days in Nice had my stomach hurting so much that I was forced to call Shanta Aunty in London to send some home-cooked food to me. She advised me to go to a Lebanese restaurant and try the pita bread and hummus. As I entered a Lebanese restaurant, I felt nauseated on seeing the meat. While eating pita bread with hummus, it felt as if I was eating bland gram curry with dry *phulka*[16]. I had somehow managed to live on hummus and pita bread for those three days. But now every time I go to London my first dinner is always at the famous Lebanese restaurant *Al-hamra* in Shepherd market.

[8 September, 2002]

[16]Wheat bread made by baking on hot plate in India

# Bribery is Widespread

Italy and France are somewhat different from the other countries of Europe. The difference between France and England can be understood through a small example. While travelling from Vienna to London, one has to cross the English Channel by ship. At Calais in France, the porters charge you a large sum of money for shifting your luggage from the train to the ship claiming that it is the standard rate. On the other hand, at Folkston, England, the porters charge only about thirty percent of what you have paid their French counterparts for the same luggage and will thank you again and again.

In our country, the practice of bargaining has decreased to some extent but in Italy and France, it is still very much prevalent. In Italy, it is common to purchase something which was quoted at a thousand lira for just five hundred after bargaining. It is not just bargaining, even tips and bribes are directly linked to a person's self-respect.

I have heard from many tourists about paying off the French authorities in order to obtain visas and passports without any hassles. An officer had once told one of my acquaintances that his face did not resemble the photograph on his passport. All it took to make the faces resemble was three hundred francs.

After the World Wars, the financial condition of France, Italy, Austria and Germany was miserable; people were broke, their self-esteem going away faster than their money. It became a common occurrence across these countries that if after buying something you did not pick your change from the till quickly, the employee would pocket it and thank you for the generous tip!

We Indians live under the illusion that English is an international language; one that is dispelled the moment you land in France. As in our country, a Tamilian speaks only Tamil even though he knows Hindi; a Frenchman will speak only in French even though he might know English. If you try to converse with them in English, they simply move away, politely saying, "Sorry, I don't know English."

Once while in Paris, I met a French girl near the Eiffel Tower. I was fascinated to see her conversing in Hindi with the Indian tourists there. She told me she liked learning different languages and had recently learnt Hindi. She was so excited about it that I did not even have the heart to find faults in her Hindi! She was at least making an effort to speak Hindi, and here I did not even know a single word of French.

Is our ignorance of the many European languages our weakness or our egotism? In one of the literary conferences I attended, I had heard a gentleman saying, "One day Hindi will be an international language." I couldn't understand what the basis of this ego was. The hard truth is - India has a long way to go before we can even hope to compete with the Europeans. We need to learn and learn and earn that status.

[15 September, 2002]

# Latin America

One more flight! But this time, I was travelling to Latin America! Comprised of Argentina, Brazil, Chile, Peru, Bolivia and Venezuela, this South American continent was my next destination for the sixth World Youth Conference, which was being organized over a week in Buenos Aires, the capital of Argentina.

I wanted to stay back after the conference and visit the other South American countries, but the visa application for each of the countries was a tiresome process as all the embassies were in Delhi only. After two months of shuttling between Delhi and Kolkata and endless efforts on my travel consultant Pawan Jaju's part, I got all the papers less than a week before the conference was to start.

I was scheduled to board the Swiss Airways flight the same night but by afternoon it seemed that I might have to change my reservations as the Venezuelan Embassy had decided to withhold my visa for some other enquiries. They had already returned my passport thrice for want of some document or the other. I called the officer as my last resort and surprisingly, my request worked and my visa was processed by the evening.

Early next morning, as I was coming out of the Zurich terminal, I spotted a gentleman in glasses and a dark brown Jodhpuri suit. Following him was an officer of the Indian Army and three female Swiss officers. It took me a few moments to recognize the then Defence Minister of India, George Fernandes, as he was wearing a dark brown suit instead of his usual collared khaddar kurta. I waved to him with a smile as we crossed each other. Returning my wave, he exited the terminal accompanied by the Swiss officers.

As there were still five days left before the conference, I decided to spend some time in London. I had always liked being in this westernized twin city of Kolkata. London had changed since my last visit some eight years back. The St. James Court Hotel, where I was staying, used to be a part of the Taj Group of Hotels the last time I was in London. The management had since then transferred to the Crowne Plaza Chain of Hotels. The hotel had an Indian owner, Indian food and a lot of Indian faces. The employees of Air India also stayed in the same hotel as did the Indian cricket team, which I realized on seeing Sachin Tendulkar in one of the elevators.

[22 September, 2002]

# Bengal and Argentina Have Old Connections

Argentina is the eighth largest nation of the world. It is said that there are four kinds of nations in the world – the developed, the developing, Japan and Argentina. While the developed and developing are classified fairly simply, there is no one who understands where Japan and Argentina stand. Japan has nothing, yet it is the world's coronet and Argentina has everything but is still a pauper.

In a way, Argentina was connected with verdant Bengal. Argentina's Embassy was in Kolkata till 1924, when it was shifted to Mumbai. Not only that, the soul of Bengal, the great poet Rabindranath Tagore also had deep relations with Argentina. After being awarded the Nobel Prize in 1924, Tagore was going to Peru by ship to attend a conference. On the way, he fell ill and at the advice of the doctor he stayed at Argentina to rest. When a very wealthy lady of Argentina, Victoria Ocampo came to know about this, she brought him to her house with due respect. Victoria Ocampo was respected all over Latin America. This lady was the daughter of a very wealthy, glorious and influential family of Argentina. She had dedicated her entire life to literary activities and was the editor of the literary magazine *Sur*.

Tagore stayed with Victoria Ocampo for about two and a half months. It is said that she looked after Tagore extremely well and influenced by that, he composed the poem *Vijaya*. During his contact with Ocampo, Tagore drew many sketches, which were later exhibited in the art galleries of Paris.

In Buenos Aires, when I expressed my desire of seeing the house, where the great poet had stayed, to the then Indian ambassador, Mr. Nigam, he immediately made arrangements to get me the required permissions.

This house is in San Isidro, Cordoba, about an hour's journey from the city. It has been taken over by the UNESCO and I was very pleased to see that it was very well maintained.

On seeing Ocampo's palatial house in the city, I was rather surprised that she squandered away all her wealth in promoting new litterateurs and artists while her own sister died without any treatment. After Ocampo's death, a trust was set up in her name which is now managed by her secretary, Maria. In 1970, when Indira Gandhi visited Buenos Aires, she had a stone plaque put up in the house to mark its significance.

As great was my happiness on seeing the foreigners take care of that house like it was national treasure, greater was my sorrow on seeing Gandhi's statue in Buenos Aires in a state of dereliction. To honour India, the Argentinean Government had named a road "The Republic of India Road". A statue of Mahatma Gandhi was installed there. I found it strange that not one person could direct me to the statue. It was almost as if it didn't exist. The reason for this ignorance became clear when I saw the statue. A black stone statue of Mahatma Gandhi had been placed on a cemented platform which looked as if it had never been painted. The cement was crumbling and there was no inscription, no plaque, not even Gandhi's name. Seeing the dilapidated state of the monument, I felt that maybe we weren't worthy of the honour that Argentinean Government had bestowed upon us.

[29 September, 2002]

# Hunger Makes a Man Unpatriotic

Argentina has suffered major economic meltdowns in the years gone by. Until 1991, its currency was Austral when the then President changed the currency, issuing Peso, which was equivalent to a thousand Australes. At that time a thousand Australes made approximately one American dollar. Hence, one Peso was considered equivalent to one American dollar. It was that one mistake which completely destroyed the country's economy. After continually paying foreign reserve, when the country broke out of its dream, the exchange rate for an American dollar had risen to four Pesos.

Banks were left with nothing. They refused to pay not only the balance of foreign companies but also the savings of the ordinary public. How could they return the money, when they did not even have money to pay their employees' salaries? After a complete breakdown that lasted eight months, the banks told their customers that they could not return their money. If the customers wanted, they could take bonds, which are a kind of receipt, for their money. When the banks would have the money, they would pay it back, whether it took five years, five hundred years or five thousand years!

Even till date, government employees in Argentina have to deposit their salaries in the banks and they do not have a right to withdraw money beyond a certain limit. That is to say that a person does not have any right to even his hard-earned money.

Due to the economic ruin, trade had closed off. Industrial institutions were shifting to Brazil. Property prices had dropped so low that the Argentinean emigrants, who had bought property in countries like Panama, sold off their lands and returned home to buy property there. Bank accounts, credit cards, deposits, everything was sealed. No one deposited money in bank anymore. But it was the government employees who had the worst end of the bargain as they did not receive salaries for many months because of sealed accounts.

Such was the situation in spite of the country having many valuable resources. Argentinean leather is famous across the world. Meat is exported in a great quantity. The value of land is not determined on the basis of its crop produce but on the basis of the number of animals it can hold for meat. Due to the miserable economic condition of the country, crime had crossed all limits. Cases of snatching, kidnapping and ransom were increasing day by day. The situation had become so bad that on the first day of the conference, one of the organizers told me very politely, “Please deposit your Rolex watch at security, sir. It is not safe to go out wearing it.” On seeing the conditions there, I understood why the organizers had requested a change in the venue when it was decided at the last Youth Conference in Jerusalem. Even before reaching Argentina, the organizers had told us that we should take only radio taxis. The local taxi drivers should not be trusted as they could be members of the mafia. As a result, on reaching Buenos Aires airport I had to wait for five and a half hours before my radio taxi showed up. The citizens were frustrated with the condition of their country, but what could they do to bring a change? The whole city was living under the shadow of fear and terror.

During the inaugural dinner, Ms. Mariglan, the then Secretary of the welcome committee of the organization had said, “I love my country very much. I believe that the conditions will certainly improve even if it all seems a little bleak right now.” Mariglan worked in the education ministry and had not received her salary for five months. She was offered work in Europe, which she refused, not wanting to leave her country and would go to the office everyday hoping to get her salary. I could feel the pain of Argentina in her voice. Turning away from the moist eyes of Mariglan, when I looked at the turbulent river from the window of the dining hall, I was reminded of the lines from Neeraj’s poem:

*Bhookhe pet ko deshbhakti sikhane waalon,*

*Bhookh hi toh insaan ko gaddaar bana deti hai*[17] .

[6 October, 2002]

[17]Neeraj has questioned the loyalty of a man under duress, citing that hunger can turn the most patriotic man into a traitor.

# Three Presidents in Two Weeks

As bad as the economic conditions were, the political scenario was worse. Congress had changed the president of the country five times in two months; three presidents within two weeks at that. Area wise Argentina is the eighth largest nation of the world, not much smaller than India; but its population is just about three percent of our population. Argentina hosts a sizeable Indian community and exports oil to many Indian companies.

Over the course of my week-long stay in Argentina, I had the opportunity to meet many well-established Indians. One of them was writer-poet Premlata Verma. Premlata was born and brought up in Uttar Pradesh before she moved to Buenos Aires where she had been teaching Hindi at the state university. She was an admirer of Rajendra Yadav, Vishnu Prabhakar and Prabha Khaitan and had followed their works very closely. When I had called Premlata, she was overwhelmed and was pleasantly surprised at finding someone speaking to her in Hindi and immediately took time out to meet me.

Premlata visited Delhi frequently and had some really good friends in the literary community there. She has translated many famous Spanish books into Hindi. She was very excited on meeting me as she would be able to send all her letters and new writings that were to be published in India through me. Her earlier letter had not reached the recipients even seven months after she had sent them. So as a parting gift, I was given about eighteen letters and some new articles for friends, family and colleagues back home.

Premlata's efforts of spreading Hindi for so many years, in spite of living in a foreign country are surely praiseworthy. She was quite unhappy with the Indian government, the Department of Culture and Languages of India and the Indian Embassy. She had been chasing them for almost a year to get a Hindi typewriter, but to no avail. In her words, "On the one hand, the Government says they want to promote Hindi and on the other hand I have to write the material with hand, get it photocopied to give to my students."

While in Argentina, I also had the opportunity to meet Manoj Mengani, a handicraft and spice trader from India. He was also the owner of Argentina's premier Indian restaurant, *Kathmandu*. When I reached *Kathmandu*, I was pleasantly surprised to see a two-storey restaurant, seating around two hundred people, excellent old Shekhawati furniture, paintings from Kishangarh, beautiful wooden elephants, Jodhpuri doors, Bikaneri chandeliers and the very welcome tune of *Banna re Baga mei Jhula...*[18] playing in the background.

Mr. Manoj Mengani told me that an Argentinean diplomat, who had fallen in love with Rajasthani art, brought all this furniture and paintings etc. while coming back from India and built this restaurant and had named the restaurant *Kathmandu* because of his love for the mountains. When that diplomat was transferred, Manoj bought the restaurant from him with all the furnishings. I was pleasantly surprised to see this miniature Rajasthan created in the *Kathmandu* of Argentina.

[13 October, 2002]

[18]Famous Rajasthani folk song

# Unparalleled Is the Tango Dance

With Argentina, comes football; and with football, Maradona. Diego Maradona brought Argentina to the centre-stage in the world of football. Who would have thought that the youngest among seven siblings in a poor family, Diego would get the honour of being the ace footballer of the twentieth century!

One more person Argentina is famous for is Carlos Gardel, the man behind the tango. It is said that every day he sang better than the previous day. There is controversy about the birth of Carlos Gardel but most people believe that he was born in 1890 in Toulouse, France. Not much is known about his childhood. But, by his teenage years, he had started singing in the cafés and pubs of Buenos Aires. Since then every child of Argentina has known him. His fame spread when he started singing on the radio in 1917. By 1928, the whole of Europe and America had become crazy about this new dance form and Carlos' voice. Some of his most celebrated works include *Por una Cabeza*, *Colver* and *Cuesta abajo*.

In the centre of Buenos Aires is an excellent restaurant - *Esquina*. Built on Al Chanta Cuatro Street, this restaurant is dedicated to Carlos Gardel and the tango. Pictures of Carlos Gardel, displays of his clothes etc., bright lights, excellent furniture, waiters wearing clothes with the name of Carlos Gardel, stewards wearing neckties with his name and a wonderful moving stage clearly showcases the Argentineans' love for tango and their devotion to Carlos Gardel. It is considered to be one of the most expensive restaurants of the world. One has to get their table booked at least one month in advance and it caters only to the tourists. People living in Argentina are not allowed there since they want to show the art of tango to foreigners.

The conference organizers had booked the restaurant for dinner on one of the evenings for all the delegates. Dinner in *Esquina* goes on from late evening to the wee hours of the morning. A film on Carlos Gardel is shown and there is a beautiful performance of tango. In three hours, not once did we feel that there was any dissonance between music and rhythm, between rhythm and tempo, between tempo and the modulation of voice or between the modulation of voice and the beat of steps.

[27 October, 2002]

# World's Third Biggest City

When I de-boarded the Varig flight at the Sao Paulo airport in Brazil, I came to know that, that day i.e. 7th December, 2002 was the Independence Day of Brazil. Brazil did not have to fight for its independence like we did, nor was there any bloodshed. But freedom is after all freedom. Sao Paulo is the third biggest city in the world and the biggest city in Latin America. Although the capital of Brazil is Brasília, Sao Paulo has become the major city from the point of view of industry and trade.

Another important city of Brazil is Rio. On the beaches of Rio, tourists enjoying typical Brazilian food are in plenty. The main language spoken here is Portuguese. If you know Spanish, you can manage but it is not only difficult but almost impossible to survive depending only on English.

It was on a Saturday that I reached Sao Paulo and above all, Independence Day. The whole city was closed. As soon as I reached the hotel, I called the Indian Consulate. They were open as they had prior intimation about my visit and that I was going to stay in Sao Paulo over the weekend. Within ten minutes, I had reached the Indian Consulate. I could not meet the Consul General but the person who had received my phone call, was waiting for me. I came to know that in Brazil, besides Brasília, the Consulate is only in Sao Paulo and Rio has an honorary consul.

Brazil has a small Indian community. On the occasion of India's Independence Day, the Indian Consulate had celebrated a ten-day festival named India-Brazil Mangalam, in which Kerala's famous painter - Karunakaran's paintings were exhibited at the local Portal Art Gallery.

Ketan Mehta's *Mirch-Masala* and Mrinal Sen's *Ek Din Pratidin* were also showcased as part of the celebrations along with other cultural programmes.

I was surprised to know that Indians had not shown much interest in the festivities. But the Indians living in Brazil are scattered. There is no particular organization to bring them together, not even for Holi or Diwali. An employee at the consulate told me, that it wasn't for lack of trying; the people were just so busy with their jobs, that no one had the time for such gatherings.

[3 November, 2002]

# But Indian by Heart

Brazil is best known for coffee and stones. In spite of a small Indian community, there are plenty of Indian restaurants there - *Ganesha*, *Agra* and *Tandoor* being the most prominent. But *Tandoor* was the only restaurant with an Indian chef, who had migrated from Delhi and cooked as your mother would. The owner of the restaurant, Lakhi Daswani was one of the more prominent Indians living there. While I was eating, Mr. Daswani came to meet me.

Daswani was related to a family in Mumbai. Being the youngest member in the family, he was sent to a relative in Africa to work. Constantly punished and unhappy with his life, one day, the ambitious Lakhi ran away from home and went to London. He went on to move from city to city, doing all kinds of work, until he finally settled in the free zone of Brazil, Manaus and started importing and exporting handicrafts from across the world. He took an immediate liking to Brazil and never looked back.

In spite of living in foreign lands for most of his life, Daswani had great love for his roots. He told me that *Tandoor* was not a commercial establishment. He had more than enough saved up to live luxuriously for the rest of his life and his one desire was that Brazil should have at least one Indian restaurant. With this thought, he had started *Tandoor*, which now boasts of tremendous following all over Latin America.

Laughing boisterously during meals, he said that it did not matter that he had a Brazilian passport or he was a Brazilian or his children were Brazilian; he was an Indian at heart, and nothing could change that.

[10 November, 2002]

# Hey Ram!

When I returned home after my month-long foreign trip, I read in the papers that on Gandhi's birth anniversary, his statue had been destroyed in Meerut. What kind of present was this to the proponent of non-violence on his birthday, by his countrymen in his own country? What kind of gift was this?

During my travel to Africa, I had developed a feeling of reverence for Gandhi. A man, who got so much respect all over the world, one whose ideologies everyone is attempting to follow, is definitely worth appreciating.

It has been our mentality that we only learn to appreciate something when the west appreciates it, even if it is one of our own. But in the case of Gandhi, the more respect his ideologies seem to be garnering from all corners of the world, the lesser they seem to be impacting in our country. I had developed true devotion to him and faith for his views during my visits to Africa and Latin America.

In the capital of Venezuela, Caracas, there are four metal statues of Gandhi. Opposite Hotel Sheraton in the residential area of Santiago, the capital of Chile, there is a piece of land named Plaza-de-India. In one corner of this Plaza-de-India, behind a spring in an enclosure, one can find a smiling Gandhi sitting between Nehru and Tagore.

Once while having breakfast with the Indian ambassador in Chile, I referred to Gandhi's statues in Latin America and the devotion the people had for the man. He told me that it was nothing compared to Chile, where there were Gandhi's statues in three of the biggest cities of Chile besides its capital, Santiago. What was most surprising to learn was that those statues of Gandhi had not been installed by the Indian Government or Embassy or any Indian organization. They had been installed at the request of the people. The Ambassador showed me a letter of the mayor of Rancagua, a small town hundred kilometres from Santiago, requesting to have Gandhi's statue installed in his city. I was happy to know that the order for making that statue was given to a sculptor of Bengal.

In Meerut whosoever may have broken the statue and whatever may have been their intention, it does not in any way reduce the respect or importance of Gandhi.

[17 November, 2002]

# Being Vegetarian in a Foreign Land!

At times it becomes very difficult for vegetarians to satiate their hunger in a foreign country, though now almost all the famous cities of the world have Indian restaurants. Nowadays, Indian clothes and Indian food are trending in foreign countries just as Chinese, Italian, Thai or Lebanese food in India. But the problem is that it is the non-vegetarian food that is most popular. I have often been asked how I managed to remain a vegetarian despite my vast travels. People even say behind my back that I only pretend to be a vegetarian citing my non-religious temperament as the reason for their claims. But my vegetarianism has nothing to do with my religion, or lack thereof. I just did not feel like giving up vegetarianism due to my family culture. That is just how I was brought up.

The only place I faced food troubles was South America. It was known as the continent of meat after all. Also, vegetarians there ate eggs and fish. So a vegetarian meal there would mean fish cutlets and omelettes. To facilitate international travellers, the airlines had started classifying food into four categories instead of the usual two: Vegetarian - that included egg and fish, Asian vegetarian, Vegan and Indian vegetarian. Some air services also offered a Jain meal i.e. Indian vegetarian without garlic and onions.

Brazil's Varig Airways and Peru's Air Peru had expressed their inability to serve Indian vegetarian food at the time of booking itself. While travelling through the countries of South America I mostly had to survive only on brown bread and coffee.

Tired of eating fruit, milk and cornflakes for four days, when I saw white rice in a big plate in a glass display window at a shop, I bought a packet of rice without thinking what I would eat it with. While paying for the rice, I tried to find out the reason for the grains being so large, white and shiny in my broken Spanish; I was shocked to learn that the rice grains were greased with beef oil. But the worst experience I had was when I went to see Machu-Picchu, the old civilization of Peru. When I did not get anything except apples for two days, I bought a vegetarian sandwich, removed the pieces of fish, washed it clean with milk and ate the bread. I feel nauseated even thinking of that now. But I figure, it was still better than dying of hunger.

[24 November, 2002]

# A Beautiful Polarization

Another important country of South America is Venezuela. Located in the upper part of Latin America, it is bordered by Brazil, Colombia and Guyana. Situated on the equator, Venezuela has two seasons - winter and summer. There are heavy rains during winters and bright sunlight during summers. And it does not just rain for a month or two; it rains continuously for six whole months. The summer heat is so severe that the rivers dry up and the groundwater level reduces considerably.

This country has the resources of becoming the biggest exporter of oil in the world, but in reality, it is on the verge of bankruptcy. Immediately after President Chavez gave up his seat, the rate and the speed at which the currency of Venezuela devalued was historical. With the fall of President Chavez, the republic too fell and is now dirtier than ever.

The public is divided into two sections, the bureaucrats and the opponents of the system. What is surprising is that both the sections are dissatisfied. Both the sections are involved in demonstrations against the public and the government respectively.

What can be said about this country? There is a lot of diversity; not only in terms of geography but also in economic and social terms. It has great wealth of natural resources, adequate quantities of minerals and many mines of precious stones that are yet to be discovered. The country has the Caribbean Sea in the north and the Amazonian forests in the south. At one end of this country are snow-covered hills and at the other, the Falcon desert, where there are beautiful sand dunes, which are known as Los Mednos de Kora.

From East to West, the plains are used for agricultural purposes. In the Amazonian region, there is the world's highest waterfall, Salto Angel but even then, there are only a few tourists. It is a matter of great concern that the tourists have no curiosity to see the world's highest waterfall. The responsibility for this lies with the government, not the tourists. There is neither any information nor resources or facilities for the tourists and the officials do not seem interested.

In the capital of Venezuela, Caracas, one of my acquaintances, Pramod Lunawat, who is of Indian origin, had said "This country has two seasons – six months winter and six months summer. In winters, clouds pour down torrential rain and in summers the sun dries up the water sources."

Even before knowing about this place from Lunawat, in Lima, another acquaintance had said that until a couple of years ago, thirty or so families of Indian origin had lived there but only two or three families are left according to the official records of the Indian Embassy. Due to economic ruin and pauper-like conditions of trade, the only Indian restaurant *Sheesh Mahal* was forced to shut down last year. I do not know why this country does not have money in spite of having enough resources. Our elders were right in saying, "Earning money is not the difficult part; saving money is."

A few years ago, when Caracas had become the trade centre of this continent, who would have thought that one day building after building would be vacant and offices would have shifted to New York or Sao Paulo?

One can assess the miserable condition of this country at Caracas Airport itself - stink from garbage piles, long queues of about three hundred people to pass through customs, getting your luggage two hours after the arrival of the plane with a broken handle, locked toilets and bullying porters with the intention of looting foreigners reflected in their eyes was what greeted you. All these things force you to wonder if this is the foreign land that Indians keep on dreaming about. Our country, dominated by rural areas is much better than such a country. Whatever may be the conditions, at least in villages, one does not have to lock their houses even today. We may not have grand airports but the weary travellers can at least get water at every few paces.

While returning to the airport, I was thinking that this was perhaps the first country, which I did not feel like visiting again. I had argued to get a one-year visa at the Embassy of this country, but two days were enough to see this almost dead country that is otherwise robust and has all the resources.

[1 December, 2002]

# Strange World – Unusual People

Last Sunday, I had an invitation from Sumermal Surana for lunch at the horticulture garden. He had organized this lunch on the occasion of the birth of twin sons to his daughter. While congratulating him on the birth of twin grandsons, an incident during my recent trip flashed before my eyes.

Rio is an important city of Brazil from the point of view of tourism. After exploring the magnificent, lively beaches, I landed at Sao Paulo Airport at 9 AM, where I had a six-hour wait to take a plane for Lima, the capital of Peru. I kept my luggage in the American Express Lounge of Sao Paulo Airport and after covering it with my overcoat, I requested a Brazilian girl dressed in a black overcoat who sat smoking nearby to take care of my luggage for a few minutes. Having seen a boarding pass for the flight after mine in her hand, I thought it would be all right to trust her. From her expression, I realized that she did not know English. I explained to her through gestures that I wanted her to take care of my luggage for a little while.

Assured by her nod, I stepped out to make a call. Our mobile phones did not work in Latin America and one had to use the phone booths to make calls. On reaching thc booth, I camc to know that I could use neither a credit card nor dollars to use the phone. It could only be used with Brazilian coins. After exchanging a traveller's cheque at the bank and making a phone call, I returned to the lounge.

By then about an hour had passed. The Brazilian girl was drinking a diet coke. As I extended my hand towards my overcoat, she grabbed my hand and started shouting. I was stunned and realized that she was objecting to my taking the luggage. The lounge manager came over to investigate all the shouting. On hearing me speak in English and the girl in Portuguese, he told me that according to that girl, another passenger had asked her to take care of the luggage and that I was trying to steal it. My mind stopped. I was in a foreign land, with a huge language barrier and to top it all, my passport and air ticket were in my overcoat, which I had left along with the luggage. I understood why everyone had always advised me to keep my passport on me at all times.

Once again I told her that it was I, who had asked her to take care of my luggage. When I reached for my luggage again, that girl dialled a number on her mobile and started shouting in Portuguese. The lounge manager's expressions were enough to tell me that things were going sour. Within five minutes three policemen arrived there. The English of the three policemen was as good as my Portuguese. With the help of the lounge manager, the police heard mine and the girl's versions. I was thinking fast as to what evidence I could give them to prove that it was indeed my luggage.

Just as I turned to the other side, I saw the Brazilian girl coming from the opposite side, smoking a cigarette. Immediately, I looked back and found a girl with a diet coke in her hand talking to the police. Both had exactly the same physique, wearing the same kind of black overcoat and had the same features; the only difference was that one had a cigarette in her hand and the other, a diet coke. They were twins – Ishaka and Vishaka. The one, who I had handed over my luggage to, gave the responsibility of looking after the luggage to her sister, Vishaka, who had come after I had left. Then Ishaka went to buy cigarettes. The girl, who had called the police, was the other sister, Vishaka.

The police, co-passengers in the lounge, the lounge manager and I were surprised and smiled. Both the sisters apologized many times. I thought no one would ever believe this incident. Hence, in lieu of forgiveness, I requested them to have a photograph taken with me without their black overcoats so that they could be identified separately in their differently coloured jackets.

In this strange world, there are unusual people. Ishaka and Vishaka were two separate personalities with the same face, but in our society the same person wears many masks, different inside and outside.

[8 December, 2002]

# On One Side the Geeta, On Other Side the Quran

I had to go to Geneva to participate in the 183rd meeting of the working committee of WFUNA. I was supposed to fly from Kolkata to Mumbai and then onwards to Geneva. After checking in at the Kolkata airport, as I turned towards the lift to go to the Club Class Lounge of Sahara on the first floor, I saw two commandos standing on either side of the lift with their machine guns. For a second, I looked into their eyes that shone like a tiger's and closed myself in the lift. I understood the reason for their presence as soon as I entered the lounge. Lata Mangeshkar, the Nightingale of India was sitting there with some people. On seeing her, my hands automatically came together to greet her.

Since I was a regular at the Sahara Club Lounge, the Lounge Manager knew me. She introduced me to Lata*ji* and the other people there in very flattering words. Lata*ji* had come to Kolkata to participate in a programme at the Netaji Indoor Stadium and was going back to Mumbai by Sahara airlines. Her niece, Ruchira, Dona Ganguly – the wife of the cricket star, Saurav Ganguly and Kavita Krishnamurti were with her. After formal introductions, I settled down in a sofa in a corner of the group.

Dona Ganguly told me that her dance school has been running for the past two years but she had decided that come what may, she would get it inaugurated by Lata Mangeshkar. Dona Ganguly had come to the airport to express her gratitude and to see Lata*ji* off.

On the plane, in the first row, the left window seat was vacant and I had the aisle seat and to the right, on the aisle seat was Lata Mangeshkar with her niece, Ruchira on the window seat next to her. I requested Ruchira that if Lata*ji* did not have any objection, I would like to interview her. She asked Lata*ji* and she nodded. Thanking her, I exchanged seats with Ruchira so that I could put questions to Lata*ji* properly.

Having started this thrilling journey with Lata Mangeshkar, when I was about to land at Geneva, I came to know that the temperature outside was three degrees. Just thinking about it made my teeth chatter.

On entering Hotel Drake after reaching there by taxi, I saw an Indian face, elderly, grey hair, salt and pepper beard and wearing a well-tailored suit. Smiling, he extended his hand, "My name is Iqbal Chisti; I am from Pakistan."

I will not lie; on hearing the name Pakistan, warmth vanished. Then I came to know that Mr. Chisti was the secretary of Pakistan's United Nations Associations delegation. That year, Pakistan had applied for the membership of WFUNA and was to be formally accepted in the 183rd meeting of the executive committee.

With Mr. Chisti, there was another man, Muhammad Bashir. Mr. Chisti was one of the well-known industrialists of Pakistan and had all political and social departments within his reach. On the very first day in the meeting, he said that his motive of taking the membership of this organization was to strengthen the ties between India and Pakistan. Later that night, while we were all having dinner at the *Shahi Hind-Pak Restaurant* he said with moist eyes that he had earned a lot in his life. He had no desires left. If for establishing friendship between these two countries, he even had to sacrifice his life, he would not hesitate. While inviting me to Pakistan, he went on to tell me about his plans and proposed friendship programmes; and in my mind, an Urdu verse was echoing:

*Ab to ek aisa warq mera tera imaan ho*
*Ek taraf geeta ho jisme ek taraf quran ho*
*Kaash aisi aman muhabbat ho hind-pak mein*
*Hamaare ghar vrat ho to unke ghar ramzaan ho* [19]

[15 December, 2002]

[19]Now let there be such a page that is mine and your faith
Let its one side be the Geeta and the other side, the Quran
I wish there is such peace and love between Hind-Pak
If there is fast in our house, they have Ramzan in theirs.

# Is It Affluence or Devastation?

It was wedding season in Kolkata. Every wedding seemed to be participating in a competition. The hosts were in competition and so were the guests. I often wonder, what kind of a social system are we a part of? A system in which the wedding of a daughter is a burden and cause of tension for every father. A father who has the capacity of spending five lacs on the wedding, wants to spend seven lacs[20] ; one who has the capacity of spending fifty lacs, wants to spend eighty lacs, and the one who can spend thirty crores[21] is adamant to spend ninety crores.

Is it affluence or devastation? Also at a time when the whole city was going through recession and businesses were on the verge of losses! Factories were closing left, right and centre. It had become difficult to make ends meet for normal people. Every day one or the other family was declaring bankruptcy. But you would never see any recession in weddings. There are always over a hundred kinds of dishes – added to that, nowadays the stalls of Italian, Lebanese, Mongolian and Japanese food are put up.

Recently, Geeta Piramal had written in a column of an established newspaper that the Marwari community that used to be the precursor in trade and business had not contributed even two or three percent to the progress in the area for many decades. The condition of big business families was shaky. Earlier people used to do transactions worth lacs and crores verbally on faith, now the lender has to keep running after the borrowers to get his money back. Forget about the interest, one has to be satisfied to get just the principal amount. Is it the same community that was considered steadfast in keeping its promises?

It is said that an excess of everything is bad. Is this not the excess of declining social values and if it is not so, one is scared even to think how frightening that excess would be. In every wedding, you find the same faces, same artificial smiles, shaking of cold hands and greetings as a formality – every person anxious to make their presence felt.

Engrossed in these thoughts and facing a cold wind, I was strolling on the bridge near Lake Geneva with my hands in the pockets of my overcoat, when my mobile started ringing. It was a call from a friend of my father. His daughter was getting married at the Royal Calcutta Turf Club next week and I was asked to be in Kolkata for the wedding. Suddenly, my heart throbbed with pain, I laughed and recalling an Urdu verse, I sat in a taxi:

*Kyon dikhate ho mujhe ye chingaariyan*
*Yahaan pehle hi aag lagi hai,*
*Ye ashk, ye aansoo meri bujdili nahin dost,*
*Kucch na kar paane ki bebasi hai*[22]

[22 December, 2002]

[20] One Lac is a hundred thousand
[21] One Crore is ten million
[22] Why do you show me these sparks?
Here fire is already burning.
These tears are not the tears of cowardice, my friend;
It is helplessness of not being able to do anything.

# When You Are Not United at Home

One day in the office, after lunch I asked the office boy to get some *rosogulla*[23] from the shop at Camac Street. The boy studied in the evening classes at St. Xavier's School and worked in my office during the day. I respected him because he has been studying and working laboriously.

When I cut the *rosogulla* with a spoon, I found a strand of hair in it. I called the boy and asked him to go back to the shop and question them if that was the sample of purity of such a renowned shop. He quietly picked the plate up and after ten minutes brought another *rosogulla* in the plate.

Cutting into the *rosogulla*, I asked him, "Did you say anything to the shopkeeper?" He kept quiet. Seeing his expression, I was a bit surprised. I asked him again a little loudly, "Did you say anything?"

Very politely, he said, "Sir, if I say something, would you mind?" When I shook my head and asked him to continue, he said, "The owner of that shop and you are both Marwaris. Later on both of you would be on one side; and being a Bengali, I would suffer in between."

I was flabbergasted. It was not a big deal, but if you thought about it, it was a serious comment. What was this misunderstanding developing between non-Hindi speakers and Hindi speakers? Who was responsible for this serious discrimination? Perhaps, we ourselves were responsible for that. How can we claim to be one nation and one country when no region has one language?

In 1995 after my first foreign trip, a programme was organized in the Merchant Chamber of Commerce, Kolkata, where the editor of *Jan Sansar*, Geetesh Sharma and I had to share the experiences of our trip. A few things that Geetesh stated in his lecture are fresh in my mind even today. He had said that after going to London, he was pained to know that whereas until a couple of decades ago, there were only one or two Indian organizations i.e. Indian Association of England or London Bhartiya Samaj; since the last decade, regional organizations like Uttar Bhartiya London Sansthan and Dakshin Bhartiya Pravasi Sansthan had taken their place. As a result, Gujaratis, Tamilians, Marwaris, Bengalis, Punjabis and Marathis, all had made their own associations on the basis of their language; annihilating the existence of the Indian associations.

The fact is that as a result of insisting on blowing one's own trumpet, the whole musical composition has been destroyed. In London when there were less Indians, then there was only one non-residents' association and if we think of an even earlier time, there was the Asiatic Society of London, which represented the non-residents of all the nations of Asia. While wandering through London, I got to know of the separate programmes of these new organizations, but I never came across any programme that all the Indian associations might have organized together. The fact is that wherever we are less in numbers, we love each other. In all the countries of Latin America, there is only one non-resident Indians' organization each, which represents all non-resident Indians.

The following lines by Iqbal are relevant even today:

*Watan ki fikr kar nadaan musibat aanewali hai*
*Teri barbadiyon ke mashware hai aasmaan me*
*Na samjhoge to mit jaoge e hindustan waalo*
*Tumhaari daastaan tak bhi na hogi daastaan me*[24]

[29 December, 2002]

[23] A kind of sweet
[24] Be worried about the country, O ignorant, trouble is brewing;
Your ruin is being discussed in the skies.
If you do not understand, you will be annihilated, O Indians,
Even your story shall not be in history.

# Situation Must Change

I had been writing the Aapbeeti Jagbeeti column for over a year. I had started the series with a promise to share some incidents of foreign lands and my own anecdotes with them. A lot has happened during this one year. Something or the other happened everywhere. In a nutshell, we allowed social values to go down; lost our economic system and brought forth our selfishness to the maximum. When I had started writing this column in the aftermath of the tragedy of the World Trade Centre in New York, to which I was a witness, I had wanted to share those moments of 11th to 13th September with you. Those were the three days when the whole world had stopped. The whole year passed but the article on the incident could not be written. Many times, I thought of writing about the World Trade Centre but week after week, my writing went from Japan to Argentina and to other corners of the world and I could not write about that incident.

All through Christmas and New Year last year, the whole incident was as clearly etched on my mind as if it was yesterday; I did not go anywhere, I did not feel like going anywhere. Bloodshed and carnage are always bad in any form, at any place, in any environment and in any way. But the strange thing is that the soldier dying at the border becomes a martyr for us and an infidel for the neighbouring country and a martyr in their history is presented as a bitter enemy in ours. How can a person become a martyr in one place when he is treated as a traitor in another?

It is said that history repeats itself. But would anyone like the Godhra incident to be repeated? Would we like the World Trade Centre tragedy to be repeated? The sad truth is that we are so engrossed in the parties of Christmas and New Year that we forget that what we pay for one night of fun and revelry can provide meals to an entire village of this country. Truth is not the parties on Christmas Eve; it is that even today thirty percent of our population cannot afford two square meals a day. Truth is not the Marks & Spencer shirt costing fifteen hundred rupees, it is your peon who runs his household in that same amount for a month. The truth is not participating in the sermons of religious saints; it is the hand-rickshaw-puller, who would have to make his children go without food at night, if he went to listen to the sermons.

I have a lot of things to say, but first I would like to say what I have wanted to say for a year about those three days I spent in New York between 11th and 13th September. I was in Chile on the first anniversary of the 9/11 tragedy and was watching the commemorations on the television sitting in a hotel room in Santiago. I wondered if it was necessary to "celebrate" this frightening act in every big city of America. Homage to the dead is usually paid silently. But 11th September was marked by America as a celebration, just to show to the world what had happened to them.

I end with the lines of Dushyant Kumar:

*Sirf hungama khada karna mera maqsad nahi hai*
*Meri koshish hai ki surat badalni chahiye* [25]

[5 January, 2003]

[25] Only to raise tumult is not my purpose
My effort is that the situation should change.

# When the World Stopped Breathing

31st December, 2002: ITC Sonar Bengal Sheraton Hotel, Main lawn, Pala Ballroom, Peshawari restaurant, Coffee Shop Eden Pavilion, West View and Dumpukht – all were filled to capacity. The hotel was decorated like a bride. Every person of any standing in the city - famous industrialists, well known artists, celebrated social, cultural and political personalities as well as enthusiastic news reporters – everyone was there.

On seeing the dazzling lights, the wonderful ballet dance, the unmatched welcome of guests, the delicious food and the crowd of great personalities, I was reminded of another evening.

9th September, 2001: The banquet hall of the world renowned hotel, Waldorf Astoria in Manhattan, New York. A special category of people of New York was present there. America's richest Indian had organized the dinner. I was also present because of one of my American friends and had made plans to meet an old friend from Kolkata, Ranjan Gupta, at 9:30 PM outside Hotel Astoria.

Ranjan was my classmate in college and after that he had settled in America and established his business. Though he had insisted that I should stay at his place in Queens, but due to my prior planning and the temptation to live near the United Nations, I stayed at a hotel. There were two objectives of my stay in New York from 8th to 14th September that year. First, participating in the annual meeting of WFUNA (the World Federation of United Nations Association) that was scheduled for 9th September and second, participating in the annual meeting of the world's non-government organizations scheduled from 10th to 12th September just before the General Assembly of the United Nations.

To participate in these meetings, the Minister of Parliamentary Affairs of West Bengal, Prabodhchandra Sinha was also with me. Sinha and I had made plans to see Manhattan with Ranjan and he had come to pick us up in his car. After going around the Times Square and the avenues of Manhattan for about two hours, Ranjan dropped us at our hotel, the Millennium Plaza. Built just opposite the United Nations, this hotel is known as the UN Hotel. Around the magnificent building of this hotel, there are the various offices related to the UN and the guests staying in this hotel are also mostly related to the UN.

We had decided to meet up with Ranjan at 4:30 PM on the following day to see the World Trade Centre and the Wall Street. On 10th September, the meeting of non-government organizations of the United Nations Organizations was inaugurated with the speech of Kofi Annan, the then General Secretary of the UN. Due to long meetings throughout the day, we started at 6:00 PM instead of 4:30 PM and when Ranjan, his wife, Prabodh*babu* and I reached the World Trade Centre after seeing the bull statue at the Wall Street, it was quite late.

Prabodh*babu* commented, "Wow! What a magnificent building! It should be seen from the top." A Bengali gentleman standing nearby introduced himself and said, "It is better to come early in the morning, around 8 AM. Later on, it gets crowded. I am also coming here at 8:30 AM with a friend."

This Bengali gentleman had been living in New York for about thirty five years and was the secretary of a Bengali organization. He was also taking his Indian friends around New York. He was very happy to meet Prabodh*babu* and insisted that we should see the World Trade Centre with him in the morning. We agreed and Prabodh*babu*, Ranjan and I decided to meet in the lobby of the Millennium Hotel at eight in the morning of 11th September, 2001 so that we could reach the World Trade Centre by 8:30 AM.

[12 January, 2003]

# The World Trade Centre 2

New York - 11th September, 2001, the Millennium Hotel, 7 AM, the alarm on my phone rang, but as always I had woken up already. I turned the alarm off and fifteen minutes later, I called Prabodh*babu*'s room. He had also woken up early.

As I was getting dressed, I got a call from India's permanent Mission in New York. Prabodh*babu* and I were to meet India's the then Permanent Ambassador, Kamlesh Sharma and Deputy Ambassador Satyavrat Pal at the United Nations at 9:00 AM. Since the Indian Mission is at a distance of just five minutes from the Millennium Hotel, some officer would come on foot to take us with him. Prabodh Sinha and I were requested to be ready by 8:45 AM in the lobby. I discussed the matter with Prabodh*babu* and we decided to postpone our visit to the World Trade Centre and go straight to the Indian Mission at 8:45 AM and finish our work there. Though the officer at the Mission had very politely said that if we had any other engagements we could visit them the following day, but we thought it better to go to Indian Mission instead of the World Trade Centre.

I thought of calling that Bengali gentleman and informing him as well as Ranjan of our changed programme. But I came to know that he had already started for the World Trade Centre and did not keep a mobile phone. Poor man, he would unnecessarily wait for us! But I had no other way of informing him.

Around 8:30 AM, the doorbell rang and I came out of the bathroom to open the door. A waiter was standing there with my coffee. Suddenly there was a loud crashing sound and on turning to the window, all I could see were the clouds of smoke.

[19 January, 2003]

# The World Trade Centre 3

I could see nothing except the dark clouds of smoke. After a few moments, when the smoke cleared a little, flames of fire from the World Trade Centre could be seen from far and wide. On hearing the crash the waiter who had come into my room had rushed off to find out what was happening. He came running back to my room to tell me that a flight had crashed into one of the towers of the World Trade Centre.

It was difficult to believe but the flames visible through the glass and the black smoke were clear evidence of the fact. I said to the waiter, "Americans boast so much about themselves, and yet cannot even fly planes properly." Last night, this waiter had been asking me to migrate to America from my country.

Just then there was an announcement on the speaker of the hotel, "Stay alert. This collision of the plane with the Trade Centre is not an accident; it could be a terrorist attack." I was stunned and thought of all the worst possible situations. If the plane had struck just a little to the left or the right, the seventeenth floor of this hotel, where I was staying could not have been saved. I was extremely nervous and prayed to all the gods and goddesses together; I had not prayed to so many gods in my whole life.

I dialled the number of Prabodh*babu's* room but the bell kept on ringing. Perhaps he had gone to the lobby. I cleaned my face and reached the lift to go down to the lobby. But the lift was shut off due to security reasons.

When I reached the lobby after descending the stairs from the seventeenth floor, I found the officer from India's permanent Mission with Prabodh*babu*. They had turned pale. I told Prabodh*babu* that if it was an attack, it would be better to go to the Indian Mission. At least there we would have a sense of security among our own people. We also decided to bring our passports and tickets from the rooms. Luckily, the other lift of the hotel was working; otherwise, I would have preferred to go without my passport and ticket instead of climbing the stairs to seventeenth floor.

After taking out my passport and the ticket from the locker of the room, when I looked out of the glass, I saw a plane coming from the opposite side; it went around the World Trade Centre, turned back and collided with the other tower of the World Trade Centre from the left. I could not believe what I was seeing. I plucked my courage and ran towards the stairs. After I came downstairs, Prabodh*babu*, the officer from the Indian Mission and I rushed out of the hotel.

There was a lot of commotion on the road. With the collision of the second plane it became certain that this was not an accident, but a well-planned attack. We reached the Indian Mission almost out of breath from running.

When we reached the Mission, the people there said that we should not have come because in New York, the permanent Missions of Israel and India share a common wall. And if it was an attack by Philistine terrorists, as rumoured, the next target could be the Israeli Mission. Shrugging, we went to the office of the ambassador. His gaze was fixed on the TV. Prabodh*babu* and I also watched the telecast of the World Trade Centre engulfed in flames. The CNN reporter had been continuously repeating this incident for the past half an hour. Suddenly we saw that one tower collapsed like a house of cards. CNN reported that the Pentagon was also attacked and that for the time being, all the planes in America and Canada had been banned from landing or flying. Not only that, the information of another plane from Philadelphia had also been received. The whole world was watching this incident on TV holding their breath.

[26 January, 2003]

# The World Trade Centre 4

Immediately, I requested Venkatesh Narayan, the secretary of the Ambassador Kamlesh Sharma to contact Kolkata so that we could inform our people about our safety. Prabodh*babu* and I gave at least three or four numbers but we could not get any line. With worry, fear, and confusion about what to do and what not to do, we went to the office of the Chancellor of the Mission, Ateesh Bhattacharya. Bhattacharya is originally from Bengal and that is why he knew Prabodh*babu*. No one remembered to follow the usual formalities of shaking hands, asking about each other's well-being or offering tea or coffee. Entering the room, we politely told him that we would be obliged if he could somehow send the information of our safety to Kolkata. Just as he pressed the button of the intercom to call his secretary Vijay Khanna, Venkatesh Narayan came running and told us that a number from the ones we had given was connected through sat phone. Luckily, the phone number was of my home at Russel Street. Our servant, Dileep was on the line. Nervously, I asked, "Where is *maa*?" Hearing my nervous voice, Dileep asked, "Why, what happened? She has gone out." With that the phone was disconnected and after that no phone line could be connected in any way for three hours. The American police had disconnected all means of communication. Telephone, e-mail, public booth, satellite phone, and wireless, no means of sending any information was available.

The tower of mobile phone company, which was on the World Trade Centre, had been destroyed and the mobile services were not working in Manhattan. Bhattacharya was inspecting the security system of India's permanent Mission. He had not moved his gaze from the scenes on TV relayed from the cameras installed outside. All of us were stunned but no one had any solution. Prabodh*babu* and I were engaged in a muted conversation that by now the news must have reached Kolkata and we shivered thinking of the condition of our families on not having any news from us. There was no solution.

Suddenly Bhattacharya asked, "What happened to the Bengali gentleman, who was supposed to go to the World Trade Centre with you in the morning?" Both of us were paralyzed with fear. The gentleman had surely gone to the World Trade Centre in the morning and the terrorist attack happened while he was there. In such a situation, it was impossible for him to be alive. Neither of us said anything. The Chancellor was busy giving instructions to the security personnel using one phone or the other.

We tried to contact the people in Kolkata using at least two dozen phone-booths till the evening, but all in vain. Finally, from the card booth of the Millennium Hotel, Prabodh*babu* could only connect with Sitaram Sharma. Sharma*ji* was worried about us. Again, the line was disconnected. But we were satisfied that at least one person in Kolkata came to know about our well-being.

An evening newspaper of Kolkata published the news that Prabodh*babu* and I were in New York. Moreover, a newspaper of Delhi even published that the minister and I had a programme of going to the World Trade Centre at 9 AM; but they did not know what had happened after that.

[2 February, 2003]

# The World Trade Centre 5

By late at night the local phone services of New York were restored but international phone services were very busy. People from all over the world were calling to find out about the safety of their acquaintances in New York. We had come back to the hotel. After a lot of deliberations, we came to the conclusion that we should not go anywhere else because after this tragedy no other place was as safe as this hotel and the Indian Mission was also nearby. Though the Ambassador, the Deputy Ambassador and the Chancellor, all requested us to stay with them at their home, but we thought it more appropriate to stay at the hotel at least for that night. On reaching the hotel, when we called room service to get something to eat, after ten minutes, someone picked up the phone and apologized for not being able to serve anything due to an emergency. Without listening to anything further, the phone was disconnected.

Arun, the son of one of my acquaintances in Kolkata, Dr. Ashok Vinayakiya, studied in Chicago. Dr. Ashok had sent packets of *bhujiya*[26] for his son. We managed with that *bhujiya* and filter coffee from the machine available in the room of the hotel. Now the matter of utmost worry was whether the planes would take off the next day or not. Prabodh*babu's* plan was to go to London by the Swiss Airways and mine, by the British Airways. On 11th September till late at night, Prabodh*babu* did not sit still in his room even for two minutes. He kept pacing up and down looking worried. I tried to console him but it did not help. Around midnight when someone said that there was a bomb in the building of the United Nations, everyone rushed out of the hotel. After an hour, the police sent the people back to the hotel assuring them that it was a rumour and there was no need to get nervous. I got angry. How was it not a matter of nervousness! We were scared to death. There was no arrangement of food. There was no surety of going back and the central office of the army that boasts of itself in the world, the Pentagon had been attacked.

The whole of Manhattan had become a cantonment. All the roads leading to the United Nations building were blocked with trucks filled with sand, parked diagonally. The bridge connecting Manhattan and Queens was closed. Manhattan was completely isolated from the other areas of New York. After about 10 PM at night, telephone services connecting Manhattan to other areas were restored.

Around 1:30 AM at night, I came back to my room and switched on the TV. On CNN, there was the same scene, the same news and the same bewildering situation. Even after running around so much, I did not feel sleepy at all. Around 3 AM, my phone rang, it was from Mummy. Just listening to my voice, she started crying. I consoled her. The international phone services were restored. After Mummy, *Maa*, my secretary, some journalist friends and acquaintances from the other cities of America, Vishal Jain, Pradeep Khosla, James Firk, Arun Vinayakiya, Priyanka Sood, Seema Bhatt, everyone called and I kept on assuring everyone but I did not have any assurance in my heart.

I called Ranjan Gupta at home and it kept on ringing. There was no answer on his mobile phone also. Around five in the morning, I received his call, "Are you all alright?" On hearing my voice, he breathed with relief and said, "Somehow I will take a ferry from Queens to Manhattan and bring you to my home."

I came to know that due to a rumour of a bomb in Queens, Ranjan had left his home at night and taken shelter somewhere else. I said, "It is okay. I will talk to Prabodh*babu* and let you know." As soon as I opened the door, I saw him coming towards my room.

[9 February, 2003]

[26] Salty snacks made from gram flour

# The World Trade Centre 6

13th September, 2001 – 7 AM, the Millennium Hotel, New York. It was my seventh day in the room of this hotel. How I spent the last two days, only I know. Every moment was filled with fear and terror. Yesterday night, again due to the rumour of a bomb, we had to spend four hours on the road, so we had decided that it was better to get out of Manhattan. Both Prabodh*babu* and I thought that it was better to leave instead of living under constant fear of bombs. Around 10 AM, the officer of the Indian Mission helped us check out of the hotel and after keeping our luggage in the car of the Mission, took us to the Mission on foot.

No flight was taking off for anywhere from America. After the tragedy, the planes that were in the skies were made to land in Canada. About ten thousand passengers were stranded in Canada for thirty hours. Thousands of people were closed in the planes on different airports of the world and lacs of people were in indeterminate condition in the middle of their journeys. No one knew what was going to happen. All the airline companies had switched off their phones. One could not get any line and if one could get one, there was the same recorded message, 'Please contact after twenty four hours, all the flights have been cancelled for the time being.'

We did not know what to do. The officers of the Mission were fully responsible for the arrangement of the departure and safety of Prabodhchandra Sinha as he was a minister. There is one advantage of being with the ministers. When the Mission sent the fax of a government letter to the authorities of the Swiss Airways that the Minister's return to the country was urgent and that he needed to be given the seat in the very first flight, a similar fax with the stamp of *Ashoka Stambh* was sent to the British Airways for me. We were at least assured that if the plane services resumed, we would get a seat in the first flight out but the question was of the services resuming and the situation being normal. Since the morning of the 11th no plane had flown. That would mean that according to the rules, if the planes were flying, the passengers with the booking for the previous two days should get the seat first and our number should come after that. In the midst of confusion of what would happen and what wouldn't, Ateesh Bhattacharya told us that there was a message that the Congress leader, Natwar Singh was stranded in a plane in London for the past many hours. Natwar Singh was coming to New York to participate in some meeting of a group of government representatives and due to this tragedy, his plane was held up at London.

I had a never-before-experience of governmental work, ways, laws and formalities in those two days at the mission. At times, one feels annoyed at the governmental machinery. I can give you an example. According to the government rules, if any Central minister or State minister of cabinet level goes to another country even on a personal trip, it is mandatory for the nearest Mission of that place to pick him up from the airport and take him to his hotel, and while returning, to pick him up from the hotel and drop him at the airport. This formality is a must, whether any other facility is provided or not.

[16 February, 2003]

# The World Trade Centre 7

14th September, 2001, 8 AM, 8-12 Austin Street, New York. Yesterday night too, I could not sleep well. My mind and body were tired after running around for three days. The Mission's car had dropped Prabodh*babu* and me at Ranjan's house. Ranjan had only a one-bedroom apartment, but he had a large heart. Though the minister and I were feeling embarrassed, we had no other choice. Every hour the minister and I were calling, sometimes the Indian Mission, sometimes the airlines and at times the people in India. The air services resumed but they would first bring their passengers stranded on the way, people stuck in Canada would come to America, the passengers with bookings for the past three days would go and then only it would be our turn. The air supervisors of both the British and the Swiss companies had phoned us to tell that they had received the message from the Indian Mission regarding our travel and they would keep us informed of the situation. We gave Ranjan's mobile phone number to both the companies as well.

Ranjan suggested that we go to the Radha-Krishan temple; we could see the shrine and also have our meals at the famous shop of dosa-idli that was nearby.

Whether there is God or not, but one does feel serenity in a temple. While going to the temple, Ranjan got a call from the British Airways on his mobile, my seat was booked for the evening flight on 16$^{th}$ September for London. Prabodh*babu* was disturbed. I consoled him that if he did not get his flight before me, I would also not go.

Ranjan was making every possible effort to put us at ease. First, he took us to the temple and then took us around Queens. In the evening, we went to Hanuman temple at Hempstead run by one of my acquaintances, *Guru Ma* and took our meals prepared by her. The next day we travelled for four hours. I was surprised to see Atlantic City. The Americans have built an exact copy of the Taj Mahal. The difference is Agra's Taj Mahal tells the tale of love and that of Atlanta's, of gamblers. This *Taj Mahal* is one of the biggest and most magnificent casinos of the world.

After returning home at night, we saw a message on the answering machine from Swiss Airways that a seat for Prabodh*babu* was booked for the morning flight at 10 AM. I was more relieved than he was because I could not go before him. On the TV, Bin Laden, George Bush, the Trade Centre and speeches of the world leaders on terrorism were being telecast again and again.

15th September, New York Airport – 4 PM, there was a lot of confusion, long queues, frightened faces and crowds of passengers. One would not even dream of seeing the passengers with their luggage, sleeping at the New York airport. At first glance, it looked like a scene at Howrah Station at night. I had reached three hours before my flight. Prabodh*babu's* plane had already taken off. At the counter of the British Airways, I was told that it was not certain if the plane, in which my seat was booked, would fly; but after forty minutes there was a flight, in which there was a seat available in the centre at the back, in the economy class and since I had the ticket for the club class, I could travel in that. I debated just for a second how I would travel for nine hours to London in the small central seat of the economy class with my physique but then taking the boarding pass, I went towards the gate. The security arrangements were flawless. The American police were checking each and every coin, pen, and belt. Due to this strict regime of security, two hours were gone. All the flights were delayed. As the plane took off from New York, I fidgeted in the narrow seat. The supervisor of the plane had told me that my luggage could not go on this plane. If I had any objection, I could get down and take another plane; or, the luggage could be sent via another flight. I just closed my eyes and nodded. At that moment, I realized that every condition is better to live in, rather than death.

[23 February, 2003]

# If One Could Get over Attachment to Home

Still in my hotel room in Santiago, I was following the coverage of the celebrations and commiserations happening all over the United States on TV. The whole country was commemorating the disaster. I may be wrong and I have written this earlier as well, but homage to the dead was paid in silence but America had commemorated the anniversary of 11th September with zest. I couldn't help thinking what was the purpose of showing all this to the world? Americans did not celebrate their misery without any purpose. We all know that every step taken by this capitalist country is measured and deliberate. Was the reason for celebrating the anniversary of 11th September to create an environment against Iraq?

The CNN bulletin was being telecast in Spanish. Picking up the remote, I was making futile effort in trying to find an English channel when the phone rang. It was a call from the owner of the hotel, Suresh Goklani. He said, "If you are free, come. We'll have tea together." I accepted the invitation.

Suresh Goklani was one of the most prominent members of the Indian community in Chile and had a grand empire of many businesses, along with this three-star Hotel Majestic. The restaurant at Hotel Majestic was the only one in Chile that served Indian food. Chile's Honorary Consul JK Saraf in Kolkata had informed him of my visit.

While sipping tea with Suresh Goklani, I got to know many things about the Indians settled in Chile. In Chile, almost all the people of Indian origin belonged to the Sindhi community. Goklani Sahib was young at heart even in his early fifties. He came to Punta Arenas in the southern parts of Chile in the early 1970s. The country was then under the military rule. A few years later, he moved to Arica in northern Chile. From there he started importing electronic items of Panasonic, Samsung and Toshiba etc., till he became the dealer of Fiat, Daewoo and Christopher cars. Two decades later, he bought a hundred and twenty-five year old house with French architecture in Santiago, and Hotel Majestic was born. He kept on talking and I wondered whether it was true that without leaving your home, limited surroundings, limited thinking and crossing that line, one may progress, but one cannot reach the pinnacle.

On the occasion of a programme of the Prabha Khaitan Foundation, the famous novelist, Rajendra Yadav had said, "Only people, who leave their homes, can establish empires." Perhaps Yadav was right. If Suresh Goklani had not left his home, he would not have been the owner of such a big business empire in this country on the other side of the world.

In the evening, while driving me around the streets of Santiago in his car, he said, "I have not been to India for the past twenty years; I married a Chilean girl named Tricia, but after marriage, I changed her name to Yashoda."

He was driving at a high speed, and on the stereo, a song was playing in Hindi, "*Ek din bik jaayega, maati ke mol…*[27]," taking puffs of his cigar, Goklani Sahib was also humming along, "*…jag main reh jaayenge, pyaare tere bol.*[28]" And looking out of the window, I was thinking that perhaps in the world, only Indians are such people, who carry their culture in their hearts, wherever they may live. That is the reason for Tricia becoming Yashoda!

[2 March, 2003]

[27] Hindi song, literally translates to one day, everything turns back to sand.
[28] Continuation of the song, translated to all that would be left of you would be your memory

# Insult to Indian-ness

One evening, I was invited to a friend's party at the Calcutta Swimming Club. This club is known throughout the country for its swimming pools. I had been organizing events in the party halls for the last few years.

That night, getting out of my car, as I was proceeding towards the stairs, the receptionist stopped me and said, "Sorry, sir, but you cannot go in."

I told him, "I am going towards the party hall."

He explained, "You cannot enter the club in a *kurta-pyjama*."

I knew that in many clubs and particularly in this club, there was a restriction on wearing *kurta-pyjama*. But I also knew that this rule was only applicable on using the facilities of the club or visiting the club. Wearing a *kurta-pyjama* in the party halls was allowed. This issue had been discussed while organizing an event at Marwari Federation and I remembered distinctly that *kurta-pyjama* and *dhoti-kurta* were allowed in party halls; only shirt with *dhoti* was not allowed.

I told the receptionist again that I knew the rules of the club and that he might be mistaken. I tried calling a few people of the organizing committee but no one was home. I again argued with the receptionist that last year I came to the programmes in the club in *kurta-pyjama* and that I was not satisfied with his response.

He contacted the office. Mishra*ji*, the person in charge of this department of the club, was on line. When I told him my name, he came down to greet me as we had known each other for many years. Mishra*ji* told me that till last year, *kurta-pyjama* was allowed in party halls, but since last December, it had been banned in the party halls as well. "Still if you want…"

I stopped him mid-sentence, "No. If that is the rule, I do not think it is correct for me to enter."

In Chile, when the organization of the Sindhis had invited me for lunch, I found all thirty of them wearing *kurta-pyjamas*. When I asked them about it, they told me that since I had come from India, they were using it as an excuse to wear their Indian clothing. In a foreign country, Indian clothing means *kurta-pyjama*. In these countries, whenever there is Indian Night or *Deepawali/Holi Milan*, the Indians feel proud of wearing this outfit. Not only in Chile or Latin America, even in Durban, people do not enter the house wearing shoes. In Africa I met an Indian family, who has had no link with India for the past hundred years. And still no member of this family ate anything before morning prayers. Damn those people, who say that after going to foreign countries, Indians forget their culture and traditions! It is we Indians who are still living here who are ashamed of our culture and traditions.

In the British era, there used to be a board outside the Calcutta Swimming Club, "Dogs and Indians are not allowed." The Indians have been allowed since Independence, but perhaps the Indian-ness is still not allowed. This rule could not have been made without the permission of the organizing committee. And this is an organizing committee where even the Governor has his nominee member. If the organizing committee of the club considers Indian-ness of *kurta-pyjama* indecent, coarse and unfit to be allowed in the club, then they have no right to be called Indian.

I was very sad on seeing this insult to the traditional Indian outfit in independent India; I was sadder still about our silence even on seeing the insult of Indian-ness:

*Ujde hue chaman dekh ke ro deta hoon*
*Badalte hue mahaul dekh ke ro deta hoon*
*Rota hoon ki meri aahon ka kucch asar ho*
*Phir unhi aahon ka asar dekhkar ro deta hoon* [29]

[9 March, 2003]

[29] I weep seeing ruined garden
I weep seeing the changed ambience.
I weep so that my sighs may have some effect
Then seeing the effect of those sighs, I weep.

# Language of Love and Humanity

On the map of India, in the south, there is a straight, long state called Kerala with one side bordered by the ocean. The map of South America has a country, similar in size and shape - Chile. This country has a bounty of natural beauty, just like Kerala. Lengthwise, the boundaries of both Chile and Kerala touch the waves of the oceans.

People of Indian origin, mostly Sindhis living in this country are blessed with the most beautiful desert and the most beautiful snow-capped mountains in the world. History of Sindhis living in Chile is a century old. In the early 1900s, Bhai Haroomal was the first Sindhi to move to Chile with three of his friends. They reached there during their journey to Las Palamas. Because of his exploratory nature, Bhai Haroomal stayed at Punta Arenas - the last corner of the world. Punta Arenas itself means a point of mud. This is where, the world as we know ends. Here during winters sometimes the temperature goes down to minus thirty degrees.

In such adverse conditions also, Bhai Haroomal gradually established a chain of seventeen stores, some of which were in Patagonia (present-day Argentina) and the Falkland Islands (now Isles Malawian). Bhojrajmal, one of his closest friends, became a business associate of Bhai Haroomal.

A few years later, another established Sindhi company, Jeti Chanray set up their branch in Punta Arenas, but it was closed down after few years. In the early 1990s, when Bhai Haroomal died, his son refused to stay in Punta Arenas and sold the business to Bhojrajmal. Bhojrajmal Holachand Nandwani established the company, B. Holachand. This company later became famous as Nandwani Brothers. At present, this company is being run by his son, Dwarkadas. Dwarkadas built a temple in Punta Arenas, which is an example of Hinduism in South America.

In those days, ships used to come to Chile via America's Cape Horn. In 1981, after the Panama Canal was opened, they started taking the shorter route. In 1920, Tarachand Devendas came to Punta Arenas to settle here. His son, Mario, became the first person of Indian origin to receive a graduation degree from Chile University. I came to know about this history during my lunch with Mario.

This elderly Mario had never come to India. He did not know Hindi and found it difficult to even understand English. Mario knew only two languages – Sindhi and Spanish. Mario, who looks Chilean, is very proud of being an Indian. When I asked Mario with the help of an interpreter if he knew only those two languages, he looked at me and told me through the interpreter that he knew one more language – the language of love and humanity, which he had learnt from his father, who had brought it with him from our country.

[16 March, 2003]

# The World is Too Small

One day, I got a call from Govind Daswani from Santiago, Chile. His son was getting married in May. The bride was from a family of Pune. All the wedding programmes were arranged in Mumbai and since on the occasion of *geet sammelan*, Bengali Night was also being organized, he insisted that I must attend it. Govind Daswani was the secretary of Indian Organization in Chile and he visits Mumbai three to four times every year on business. In Santiago, his company *Namaste India* is famous for Indian goods, jewellery and handicrafts etc. His son, Kabir had shown me the whole city when I was in Santiago. Kabir's sister, Aarti was doing a research on a topic related to India at the Santiago University. Aarti had then introduced me to a young Bengali boy named Supriyo Bose. In spite of originally being Bengali, Supriyo Bose was the professor of Hindi at the Santiago University. Supriyo's family had shifted from Bengal to Agra many years ago and he alone settled in Chile. He told me very proudly that for the past ten years, Durga Puja was being organized in Agra under his family's supervision and for the last three years, he had been making an effort to organize Durga Puja in Chile also. Supriyo was married to Dolly, who belonged to a Sindhi family settled there. The credit for my visit to these far off countries, Chile and Peru of South American continent goes to Dolly Bose.

Dolly worked in a travel company *Le Travela-en* in Chile and she had prepared a well-planned itinerary for me to visit Peru's Machu-Picchu civilization, the beautiful Patagonia, the attractive Calama deserts and Caulle volcanoes. Dolly was the only person in all the travel agencies of Santiago city, who could understand and speak English fluently. When Aarti Daswani had introduced me to Supriyo Bose and he told me the name of his wife, Dolly Bose, I really believed how small the world is in spite of its immensity, disharmony and diversity.

Half an hour after taking off from Chile's Santiago airport, when I looked out of the window, I saw only dry hard earth. I have seen the deserts of Jaisalmer and Thar also from such a height. The Thar Desert looks soft and is dark brown in colour from that height. But the Calama desert looked like blackish hard stone. Though the plane was flying at a relatively low height, while descending towards El Loa Airport, Calama for ten minutes I could see only dust and infertile, hard land.

In front of my eyes, there was a sea of brown dust, completely silent and still. Extremely surprising are nature's strange ways, for all around the infertile hard land were cold snowy mountains! Snow seen on the mountains from a desert! I could not even imagine that. Calama airport is very small. From there, to reach my destination, the Maduma village, I had to travel two hundred and thirty kilometres through the desert. A young villager with a car was waiting for me, carrying a stone plaque with my name in his hand. He stopped the car near a shop and through gestures, asked me to buy water, cold drinks etc. I refused shaking my head. He bought three bottles with his money and kept them. Later on, I repented my decision. In the two hundred and thirty kilometre long journey, there was nothing except desert. If you felt hungry or thirsty on the way, there was nothing you could do about it. On both the sides, there was only dust; there was no sign of green grass or plants, creatures, shops or houses. Before turning on the road, a policeman saw my passport and asked, "Have you come from India? So far! Surprising!" I asked him, "Don't Indian tourists come here?" He answered, "This is the first Indian passport that I have seen in at least nine years. Yes, some people of Indian origin with American passports do come."

[23 March, 2003]

# Why Restrictions on Dressing?

After reading about the incident at the Calcutta Swimming Club, many people called and asked me if it had really happened, or if I was insulted. Many people also said that they had also been to the party hall in *kurta-pyjama* and that the gate keeper must have been mistaken. I had to explain that this restriction on wearing *kurta-pyjama* in the compound of the Calcutta Swimming Club had been imposed very recently and that I wasn't insulted. The only thing that I had in my mind was whether it was right. And I wanted to ask my dear readers - does the *kurta-pyjama* have no right to be accepted in civil society? Admittedly, the Calcutta Swimming Club wanted to protect its English legacy, but I was extremely surprised when a lady member of the executive committee of the Hindustan Club, which claims to be completely Indian, traditional and cultured said to one of my friends, "From next month, we will also impose a restriction on wearing *kurta- pyjama* in the club."

I could not believe it. I called her and she said, "Now that the new building of Hindustan Club is ready, we are also going to ban wearing of *kurta- pyjama* in the club."

I could not say anything to her. The Marwari community considered the club as its own and in the whole city, the Hindustan Club is considered to be the club of Marwaris and Gujratis. Our elders associated with this club have started putting in an effort to save our culture.

We hear and read that those who live in India are Indians i.e. Hindus, Muslims, Sikhs, Christians, all are Indians. The outfits for all the castes and sub-castes, even before the British rule, were *dhoti-kurta* or *chhadar-pagri* and even today, we see our leaders wearing *dhoti*, *kurta* and jacket. If we go deeper into layers of society, we find that *dhoti-kurta* was considered the dress of the Hindus and *kurta-pyjama* that of the Muslims.

The argument given by the Calcutta Swimming Club is that there is no restriction on wearing *dhoti-kurta*. Did that mean that the restriction was only on the Muslim dress, not on Hindu *dhoti*? In North India, *angvastra* or *kor* is worn with *dhoti-kurta*; or, *sherwani*, *achkan* or jacket is worn over *pyjama-kurta*. In Kolkata, people go to weddings wearing *kurta-pyjama* or *dhoti-kurta*.

The club culture was actually passed on to us by British. In the pre-Independence era, people used to go to the club in pant, shirt, coat, tie, hat and boots and they used to think that the Indians, who go there, should also follow in their footprints. Even then people wearing *dhoti* were welcomed because the land owners in Bengal used to wear *dhotis*. They had the money and hence the right to go to the club. The club was off-limits to the common man and hence, no one ever discussed the issue of wearing *dhoti-kurta* or *pyjama-kurta*.

When I think about the objection on wearing *kurta-pyjama*, I recall all the political leaders of South India, who proudly enter the Parliament wearing *lungis*. Another argument was whether one can go to the office in *kurta-pyjama*. But a club is not an office. Parties for weddings etc. are not held in offices. One goes to a club in the evening after the office. At times I think that even if the English were here today, they would have started wearing pant and coat of chiffon due to the heat. I know most of the members of the managing committee of the Hindustan Club. They must think of what message they want to give to the young generation by banning *kurta-pyjama*. Poor *pyjama!* I wonder if I should also discard it and start wearing a *dhoti*. I shall have some importance not only in the club but also in the rule of B.J.P.!

[30 March, 2003]

# ...Then I Fell Asleep

Recently on *Holi*[30], I had gone to Rajasthan to participate in a programme. There was a lot of betting on cricket. If you think about it, a person who bets is a very imaginative person. Whether it would rain or not, where water would fall from the terrace, whether the flow of the water would be heavy or light, only a person with imagination can think of such things.

It is said that the people of Rajasthan have earned a part of their wealth through betting. It is surprising to know that the betting of huge amounts goes on in every small township. Whatever be the case, whenever I come to Rajasthan, their warm, intimate behaviour touches my heart.

Rajasthan's *Holi* has its own charm. In Bengal particularly, the gaiety on festivals is decreasing. The reason is the ban on the use of crackers and colours. While going from Delhi to Churu, we were passing through the villages of Jhunjhunu, when I got a call from a Bengali dramatist, Usha Ganguli. I could not understand how my mobile was working in these remote areas. Later on I came to know that the mobile culture had spread to the villages too. In the deserts of Chile, I would often think that if in such sandy deserts, smooth roads could be made; then why not in Rajasthan. If in the deserts of Chile, there could be life even when there is not a single green leaf, the famine-stricken Rajasthan should do better. At that time, I did not know that these things would become reality so soon, and my roaming mobile phone of Kolkata would work on the Jhunjhunu-Churu road.

It was a pleasant surprise to talk to many people on mobile while sitting in the Circuit House of Churu. Admittedly we have not progressed as much as we should have after Independence, but who is responsible for that? The system, the governance or us? In Chile, Suresh Goklani had told me that within eight years of independence, more than five hundred kinds of cars had come in the Chilean market. Every person there considers it his duty to pay full taxes to the government. If we look into ourselves, we would know how much tax we pay and how much we evade. Evading is also theft. Our mentality is such that we feel proud of saving even three rupees by not buying a platform ticket. If we pay full taxes to our government, perhaps Chile and America would be insignificant in terms of progress.

The need of the hour is to be conscious. If we do not wake up now, our silence may prove to be the harbinger of a heavy storm. Forget about other countries, if we ourselves keep on allowing our insult in our own country publicly, it might be too late.

In such moments, I am reminded of Neeraj:

*Fursat to mujhe thi desh ke liye bahut*
*Par pet bhar gaya to mujhe neend aa gayi* [31]

[6 April, 2003]

[30] Festival of Hindus

[31] I did have a lot of time for my country
But when I got satiated, I fell asleep.

# I Wish Ram Chatterjee were Alive

I had anticipated the reaction to my reference to the incident at the Calcutta Swimming Club. Many Hindi, English, Bangla and Urdu newspapers had published this news of the ban on *kurta-pyjama*. The Club also fulfilled their duty by arguing in favour of the rule. The only ones, who did not fulfil their duty, are us and our society. If our society had protested against this rule, we would have been enjoying tea and snacks near the swimming pool of this Club wearing *kurta-pyjama*.

The Hindustan Club issued a press release saying that the club was not banning the Indian dress and that no such proposal had come to the executive committee for consideration. The member of the executive committee, who had said so, was referring to it informally. I still could not understand why the Calcutta Swimming Club was adamant in holding that *kurta-pyjama* is not a sign of civility?

The office-bearers of the Calcutta Swimming Club said that it was a rule being followed for decades. But this is wrong. The fact is that the restriction on wearing *kurta-pyjama* in party hall has been imposed since last November. Another argument given was that they could not allow loose *pyjamas* in the club because by pulling up loose *pyjamas* to the knees, one can indulge in vulgarity. I was astounded at the lack of faith the club had in its members. As only members and their guests are allowed in the club, did the club not trust the character of its members? As far as the question of vulgarity in pulling up the *pyjama* till the knees is concerned; then should we consider being around the pool in swimming costume also vulgar?

There is no limit to nonsensical arguments. One of the senior members even said that banning *kurta-pyjama* is saving the hundred and twenty-five year old traditional legacy of Bengal. What was this legacy of Bengal - playing cards in the club, organizing rain dances, drinking peg after peg in the bar while looking at the swimming pool? I could not understand what tradition was being saved by only banning the Indian dress?

Some people also comment that the club is a place, where its members have a right to make rules and regulations as they wish. I am sorry to say, but if you burn national tri-colour sitting in your drawing room and say that it is a personal matter, I consider it treason. As far as the club is considered, it is not personal but public property. Even technically, the Calcutta Swimming Club is the property of the Hon'ble Governor of West Bengal.

Some elders say that in 1967, Ram Chatterjee who had been a minister then, had forcibly entered the club with his goons. Only after that, were the Indians allowed to use the swimming pool. I think that if in 1967, the friends of Ram Chatterjee were goons, then such goons should be publicly felicitated.

[13 April, 2003]

# Is This Our Civilized Society?

I got a call from an established English daily saying a woman of our community has been turned out of her home with her two children. For one week, she was dependent on others for even a single morsel of food, but she could not get any shelter. On probing, it was found that her husband had forced divorce on her and since the date for signing the papers was coming closer, he had started torturing her.

This lady of Maheshwari community had been living separately for the past four months and the flat, in which she was living, had been allocated to her elder brother-in-law. The landlord and her brother-in-law forcibly threw her out of the flat at midnight. The lady approached a number of people for mediation but no one came to her aid. Even her own brothers, who lived in Assam, refused to help. She did not have parents and the police also showed their true colours.

Some people tried to take advantage of her helplessness, but no one came forward to help. If there was anyone, who extended a helping hand; it was an elderly Bengali advocate, who was fighting the lady's case pro-bono. It was due to this advocate, that the incident was reported in the English daily. I was stunned and through my sources found out about the whole situation.

The next day, the same English daily published the entire story of the lady. The whole Marwari community started talking about this. Throughout the day, phones and exchange of information continued. Some people said that it takes two to tango. Many people said that if the husband was at fault, then so was she; that she was also responsible to some extent. Some others said that, if she was unblemished, why did her brothers refuse to help? Some considered her husband's accusation of her being characterless as well as the husband's action of divorcing her correct.

Nowadays, incidents of divorce are not rare in the Marwari community. Exploitation of women keeps on happening. But the fact is that a lady with two children knocked on every door for help and food and no one helped her. Even if we accept that the lady is at fault, how is it justified to keep two small children hungry?

The next day, the midday issue of the English daily reported that there had not been any solid arrangements made for the children and if at night the advocate had not given them shelter, the lady and her children would have had to sleep on the footpath on an empty stomach.

Our conscience has been dead for so long that we do not have any sensitivity left. There are a number of organizations of Maheshwari community, the Marwari community and women's organizations claiming to support those in need. Yet, no one came forward and offered her even food and shelter. It seems that these organizations are so busy with organizing religious programmes, prayers and singing praises of god that they do not have time to stop such a big social crime. I am ashamed of myself too that I am considered one of the social workers of this society.

[20 April, 2003]

# How Can *Kurta-Pyjama* Be Vulgar?

On the inaugural *yagna* of the building of Marwari Sammelan, I saw the picture of the Chief Secretary of the Sammelan and host of the *yagna* programme wearing *kurta-pyjama*. The week before, I had gone to Auckland Park to attend a cultural programme of the Sindhi community and almost all of the people were wearing *kurta-pyjama*. This week, I had gone to attend a music programme of a Punjabi friend and the bridegroom was wearing *kurta-pyjama*.

In the procession, on the birth anniversary of Lord Mahavir, many people of Jain community were wearing *kurta-pyjama*. At the annual function of a renowned school of Kolkata, the Principal was wearing a light brown *kurta* with a white *pyjama*. On *Muharram*[32], when I went to Rajasthan, for a felicitation programme, almost all the chiefs of various congregations at the procession were in this dress. That is to say, in all religious, cultural, social and educational programmes, this dress is preferred by the people of all the religions, communities and castes. Then, how can *kurta-pyjama* be a sign of vulgarity?

Even in all political programmes, people usually wear this dress whatever political party or ideology they may belong to. In fact, one thing that is common among the people of all the religions, the political leaders and the people of different ideologies is this dress of *kurta-pyjama*. Two people of completely different ideologies – the Speaker of the Legislative Assembly, Hashim Abdul Halim and Bala Saheb Thackeray – wear only *kurta-pyjama*. That is why our national dress is *kurta-pyjama*.

Our Constitution says that insulting our national language, national song, national animal, national bird, national sport, national flag and national currency is a crime. If so, then why is the national dress insulted?

What is vulgar about this dress that one cannot go to the Calcutta Swimming Club wearing it?

A few days ago, again a national daily gave prominent space to this incident. A senior official of the Club gave a statement to the Press that our national dress is not *kurta-pyjama*, it is *dhoti-kurta*. I pity his mentality. Only something that is dear to and acceptable to all the religions and the communities equally should be considered national. I have never seen a Muslim wearing a *dhoti-kurta* till today. Muslim community has nothing to do with *dhoti*. Wearing of *dhoti* is a contribution of Hinduism. Can the officials of the Club respond why they are permitting Hindu traditional dress in the guise of nationality in the Club? Does it not mean that the dress of the Muslims is ignored at the Calcutta Swimming Club? If the Hindu *dhoti* has a right to be allowed in the Club, then Muslim *pyjama* also has this right. My motive is not to spread communalism but responding to such childish statements is also essential.

At the Taj Bengal, in a programme of Oswal community, where prominent industrialists, prominent political leaders, prominent journalists and prominent social leaders were on the stage, Acharya Kalyanmal Lodha called the rule of the Club- slavery of the English and criticized it strongly. Many people suggested that we should give a notification to the President after holding a discussion. But no one really acts.

At times I wonder whether it is better to keep quiet in front of this society that is in deep slumber. What is my status after all? The Calcutta Swimming Club would not allow even Hashim Abdul Halim, Bala Saheb Thackeray, Lalu Prasad Yadav, George Fernandes, Nitish Kumar, Ramvilas Paswan and twelve other chief ministers of this country in the club because they wear the vulgar dress, *kurta-pyjama*!

[27 April, 2003]

[32] Muslim festival commemorating death of Imam Hussain

# Peru

If you hold the globe in your hand and pierce across and downwards through India, this object will come out in Peru. Historically, this South American country is very significant. The Inca civilization started and declined here. These people, who were quite similar to Asians in their features, have been successful in saving their culture and civilization to a great extent.

When I disembarked from the plane of the Air Brazil at Lima, the capital of Peru, the weather was moist and slightly cold. Later, while driving to the hotel from the airport, I came to know that like Mumbai, Lima is situated on the shore of the ocean and there is moisture in the weather throughout the year. While abroad, when I am alone, many times I think about the similarities among the people of the various civilizations of the world in spite of the vast cultural differences!

While sitting on a small wall at the beach of Lima, when I looked at Hotel Mede Plover on the opposite side, it looked exactly the same as the Oberoi Hotel from the wall of Marine Drive at Nariman Point in Mumbai. Not only the beach, while going around in Peru, I found so many things bearing such similarity to our culture and civilization, that I was confused. A sub-caste of the old civilization of Peru, Inca is present there even today. They are known as the "Indian".

Though this "Indian" sub-caste is too small, I was very surprised to find their rituals and wedding customs to be exactly like ours. The bride fills the parting in the hair with vermilion as we do here, the ritual of circling the fire during the wedding ceremony is also like ours and even their dress is similar to the clothes of traditional *jani* of Rajasthan and the clothes that men wear in Nagaland. About four hundred villages of Peru are inhabited by this Indian caste. Their language is called Quechua. In this country, the sun, the moon, the mountains and rain are worshipped as gods even today.

These Quechua speaking people are mostly farmers. It is said that from 1000 B.C. to 1450 AD, this caste dominated Peru. Its downfall came after the attack by Spain. I was in for another surprise when I went to a temple in the city after visiting the villages. Peruvians worship a stone called Baka which resembles our *shivling* (black stone depicting Lord Shiva).

[4 May, 2003]

# Ownership of Whole Society

In Peru along with a number of similarities with our country, corruption is also equally dominant. The common man of this country is very disturbed and helpless due to corruption in day-to-day life and in the government departments. This country exports petrol and silver and major crops here are potato and maize. There are only two major cities, Lima, the capital and Arequipa. Alcohol is consumed here as cold-drink is consumed in our country. Father and son drink together very comfortably at home.

In earlier times, there were three capitals, Arequipa for the plains, Cuzco for hilly areas and Vilcabamba for areas with forests. But in 1572, after the assassination of Tupac Amaru, the last descendant of Inca royalty, this empire ended. Even today the common man of Peru hates the Spanish. The father of this nation is San Martin. San Martin is perhaps the first person, who is honoured as the father of two nations.

While visiting rural areas of Peru, I came to know many interesting facts. Here cultivation depends entirely on community cooperation. Helping each other in cultivation is called *ginni*. Knitting is common among the women. They create designs related to their rural traditions and life-style on blankets and clothes etc. Prints on the clothes are of village scenes; or flowers, leaves and rivers; or ravines or hills. The government has taken many steps for the progress of the villagers by providing special packages for education and electricity, etc. for them. The most special thing about the Peruvians is that they do not write down any information; they commit it to their memories.

Something that I found unique to this country was the farming system that was unheard of anywhere else in the world. No single person is the owner of arable land. The ownership of the land is of the whole society.

The society decided who will cultivate which part of the land and that also kept on changing according to a particular system. There was no argument, no ownership, no landlord, no one mere farmer; everyone was the owner and everyone, the labour.

I wish in our country also after the ending of the system of landlords and royal families, some similar system had been adopted so that no one was the owner of any land. Then no one would have tried to raise crops in barren land uselessly, nor would arable land in Punjab be without cultivation due to an old farmer's son getting a job in Canada.

What is the reason that every civilization and culture of the world has some aspect that is glorious? Every evening we go to a club but every morning we bow our heads in front of *Dadi Sati* [33]. On Saturday night, we visit nightclubs and bar lounges, but we take our wives with us in *sari* or *salwar-suit* only. We may go for honeymoon to the valleys of Switzerland or liberal Sweden but if we see any relatives there, we greet them by touching their feet. We go to Pizza Hut but order Indian curry-pizza. We send our children to study in a convent school and also tell them how grandpa dresses simply and eats simply. Why doesn't man adopt any one civilization fully? All the civilizations are good, whosoever they belong to, if they are adopted fully. But we are neither able to save our civilization and culture nor adopt another civilization fully.

[11 May, 2003]

[33] The faith of the Marwaris of the Jhunjhunu area.

## The Secret of the Green Concoction!

From the point of view of tourism, the most famous region of the world is Peru's Machu-Picchu. People from all over the world come to this country to see the remains of this civilization. From Lima airport of Peru, I boarded a small helicopter like plane, which could seat only seven people. After about two hours, I got off at a small airport named Cuzco among the hills.

Cuzco city is more like a big township. Tourists have to spend a night there to go to Machu-Picchu. At noon in September, the temperature was minus three degrees. Cuzco is very important from a historical point of view. This city was the capital of Inca civilization. This region with a population of approximately forty thousand is situated at the height of 11,200 feet from sea level. The major occupation here is related to tourism. The hotels are in a row. Though there are no facilities like five star hotels, the rooms available are neat and clean.

Just as I landed there, I found an employee of my travel agency standing with my name on a clipboard. Before sitting in the car, he quickly opened a thermos and gave me a bitter drink, something like green tea. When I shook my head in refusal, he said that this place was very high from the sea level, therefore every visitor must drink it every two hours to avoid breathing problems. I closed my eyes and gulped down the drink. When I asked about it, I was told that it was prepared by boiling the leaves that grew on the hills here.

When I reached the hotel passing through the narrow lanes, the receptionist gave me the same drink even before handing over the key to my room. My guide told me that I had to rest that day since I needed to acclimatize myself to the climate for at least twenty-four hours after that drink. After my visit to Cuzco on the second day, I would be taken to my destination, Machu-Picchu on the third day. I agreed to the plan, closed the door and after lighting up a fire, I snuggled in the blanket. I was actually breathing heavily, was tired as well and on the top of that, in the name of vegetarian food, I could get only tomato soup and that too made using green tomatoes. I opened the packet of Lebanese food that I was carrying with me and ate it with shaking hands. I thanked Kabir Daswani, who had got a bag of vegetarian Lebanese food - Pita, Hummus and Falafel etc. that did not get stale, packed for me at Santiago while telling me about the situation in Cuzco.

I looked at the typed itinerary, the first day, I had to rest; the second day, I was to visit famous catholic churches, San Cristobal, Santa Teresa, La Catedral, San Blos, La Compania, Santo Domingo, San Pedro and Museum, Religious Art Museum, Santa Catalina, Municipal Palace, Museo de Sitio, Regional History Museum, Popular art market, etc. After that on the third day, I was to go to Macho Mama by the morning train to see Machu-Picchu. Macho Mama means the earth, i.e. our land that is like mother.

It had not been long since the remains of the civilization of Machu-Picchu were discovered. They were discovered by an American, Hiram Bingham in 1911. During the invasion of Spain, this region was used as a secret city; hence, its civilization was discovered after so many years.

In the evening, I came to the main crossing after walking just a few paces from the hotel. Whichever way I looked, I found only tourists but forget about an Indian, I could not even see a Pakistani or Bangladeshi there. There was no one with a brown complexion like ours. It is true that we Indians live within a fixed mindset. In the name of travel, we think at the most about the valleys of Switzerland or nowadays, we are going towards New Zealand and Australia a little but this place still does not figure on our travel plans.

[18 May, 2003]

# A Suffocating Night

While walking around the main crossing of Cuzco, time and again I would glance at the restaurants by the side of the footpath with a hope that I might get something to eat. On one side, I saw a board with "Asian foods" written on it. I found out that in vegetarian food, I could only get noodles and even those were half cooked. Somehow I gulped a few noodles down with two cans of coke and came back to my hotel. The moment I entered, the waiter again handed me that tea-like concoction. Slightly angry, I refused it and turned to the stairs to my room. Though I did feel some change in my breathing in Cuzco, but it was not anything problematic. When the waiter asked me for meals, I refused.

Cuzco was the only place in the whole of Latin America, where you could live only by knowing English. The main source of livelihood of this region was tourism. Hence, English was necessary. When I refused to take the meals, the waiter helplessly said, "Sir, charges for your meals are included in the charges for the room. So you do not have to pay extra for your meals, you can have your food." First I laughed and then felt angry. I do not know why the West gives so much importance to money. Everything, every moment, every procedure is decided by money.

I remember the first time when I went to New York; I got to see a wonderful example of this mentality of the West. There is an Indian restaurant near the Indian Mission in the United Nations in Manhattan, *Maharaja*. When I entered this restaurant in the afternoon to have a meal, an American asked me in practised words what kind of meal I would like to have-one plate lunch, standing lunch or sit-down lunch. I was confused, I knew about the classification of vegetarian and non-vegetarian in buffet dinner, but I could not understand this classification of vegetarian food.

Hesitantly, I satisfied my curiosity. I came to know that there was a difference of three and two dollars in the three kinds of meals. In the one plate lunch, you pick up a plate, fill it with as much food as you want, you cannot have second serving and it costs fourteen dollars. In standing lunch-like buffet, you can take as many servings as you want but you will not get a place to sit and it costs seventeen dollars. Sit-down lunch costs nineteen dollars, for which you have the permission of sitting down to eat lunch. A waiter will serve you water and sauces, pickle etc. at your table. In other words, every little thing is accounted for.

This incident during my first New York visit is enough to explain the mentality of the West. Even if two brothers go for lunch together, they split the bill. Anyway, thinking about these things I did not realize when I fell asleep.

Suddenly I felt some problem in breathing and my eyes opened. Taking a long breath, I pressed the button to switch on the light – it was 1:30 AM. First, I thought that it was a momentary uneasiness due to altitude, but when I was coming out of the bathroom after splashing water on my face, I saw a warning sign over the switchboard which said "if your breathing is heavy, contact the reception." I got nervous. I fell down even before reaching the bed and palpitations started. I was not able to understand anything and I was worried that if something happened to me, my family would not even be able to trace me. Somehow I pressed the button of the reception and remembering god, started taking long breaths. I was feeling suffocated and my eyes closed. When my eyes opened, I found myself in the room and the clock was showing 7:30 AM. An oxygen mask was on my nose and a little sunlight was coming from the window.

Later I came to know that due to altitude, the tourists usually face this problem in Cuzco and that is why they are made to drink the concoction again and again. I did not drink the concoction, so I had to face the consequences.

I had not told anyone about this incident until now - I would like to visit some more places and you can very well imagine what my family's reaction would be had I narrated this incident to them.

[25 May, 2003]

# Eyes Sparkle with Jewellery

Peru was the last stop in my journey across Latin America. While seeing the civilization of Machu-Picchu, anybody would be proud of the intellect, sculpture as well as mental development of his ancestors. Research is still progressing on the remains of Machu-Picchu; as to which building was for what purpose, which place was the bedroom and which place was for worship and how this secret city was inhabited. Without exploring the ruins, one cannot find out all this. Hence, the tourists stay here for months together.

Not only Machu-Picchu, the Gold Museum in Lima, the capital of Peru is also very famous. If there is any place in the world with the maximum number of gold objects, it is the Gold Museum of Lima. Eyes start sparkling on seeing the golden jewellery in the entry hall of the museum.

The whole museum is the personal property of one, Miguel Mujica Gallo. This man has collected the golden objects from all over the world to make this museum. At present, his two daughters are the owners of this glorious and priceless museum. The value of all the gold in this museum has not been assessed till date. The most famous object in this museum is the golden ceremonial knife. This knife, embedded with jewels, is famous all over the South American continent. Outside the museum, in the souvenir shops, innumerable symbolic memorabilia of this knife are available.

Approximately two hundred Indians live in Peru; most of them, Sindhis and Punjabis. The most famous person of Indian origin in Peru was Arun Kapoor. When I went to the huge residence of Kapoor I could not help but be fascinated by the luxury of the place.

Arun was a very lively person. Laughing loudly with his wife, Sushma, he told me that he owned the Kamal theatre in Delhi. In 1976, he had left his home and come to Peru because his family considered him worthless. He had then set up a cinema hall with a citizen of Peru and now owned all the seventy-six cinema houses of Peru. The first film in the language of Peru was also produced by him.

Last month Sushma Kapoor came to Delhi. Speaking with me over the phone, she said that they had started planning the biggest multiplex theatre in Mumbai. But the problems they were facing for building one cinema house at Mumbai and from its government were much more than what they faced while building all seventy-six cinema halls in Peru. They said that they were building a theatre in Mumbai just as a hobby, not for business. But seeing the attitude of the government, one felt bad.

The day I met Arun and Sushma Kapoor, it was their son's birthday party at the Mary Floor Club of Lima. I met a number of Indians there. Everyone criticized the industrial approach of Indian government. Everyone believed that if Indian government gave facilities and made the ways of business easier, people like them would not have to try their luck in foreign countries.

[1 June, 2003]

# We Always Keep Quiet

I had booked a ticket in an Indian Airlines flight for travelling from Chennai to Kolkata. I had been a regular passenger of Jet Airways for many years and the service of the Indian Airlines was completely new to me, but I knew I should not compare the services of private airlines with the government owned Indian Airlines.

Having seen and experienced the functioning of the government, I have accepted the fact that we should have the least expectations from the government and we should consider whatever we are able to get from them, appropriate. But during this flight, what I saw and experienced, compelled me to write about it.

The flight from Chennai to Kolkata in the evening is an airbus, which is widely considered the most convenient. The Indian Airlines is quite proud of its airbuses because they are better in comparison to the plane services of the private companies.

After taking off from Chennai, I looked around and there was only one other passenger in the business class. Since there were only two passengers, the air hostess was also relaxed.

Halfway through the flight, there was a strong jerk and the plane lurched slightly. All the passengers were shocked. There was an announcement, from the flight deck that we were required to return to our seats and fasten our seatbelts. As I tied my seat belt, straightening my seat, the plane jerked again. At this, many passengers in the economy class at the back cried out. The plane had started wobbling.

I was used to air travel every fortnight, and could understand that sudden change in weather like lightning or thunder had caused this rocking of the plane. As I was on the first seat, I could see both the air hostesses sitting with their seat belts on. When I heard the sound of vomiting from the rear of the plane, I asked the air hostess through gestures what the matter was. The air hostess shook her head indicating that she did not know. Later on I came to know that the air hostess was not allowed to say anything without the permission of the captain of the plane.

After about ten minutes of wobbling, the plane descended with a thud and the twinkling lights of Kolkata were visible. Many passengers were sweating. The cries of many women had turned into weeping. Seeing the plane fly normally, many people heaved a sigh. The air hostess undid her seat belt and taking the box of tissue paper ran towards the lady, who had vomited. At that moment, the captain announced that the plane was landing at Kolkata.

When my co-passenger asked the air hostess if the weather was bad, she said, "Yes, perhaps…" There was no limit to my surprise. As per the rules, the captain should have made an announcement that the weather was bad, because of which the plane was shaking. I do not know why the captain did not consider that appropriate.

The plane had landed at Kolkata. It was raining outside. Many passengers were angry as to why the captain had not announced that it was just bad weather; at least then the passengers would not have been scared. The air hostesses clearly stated that they could not do anything in this situation as they had no right to make announcements; though both the air hostesses accepted that it was a mistake on the part of the captain, and that he should have made an announcement

While waiting for my luggage, I was thinking that if this incident had happened in Europe or a country like America, the passengers would have sued the airlines and perhaps got it auctioned. You would be surprised to know that all the angry passengers left after picking up their luggage. Nobody thought it appropriate to register a complaint.

In our country, people complaining against such things are called fussy, crazy or mad; whereas in other countries, people consider complaining against such things their fundamental right. The difference between them and us is clear.

I strongly felt that I should send a fax to the office of Minister of Civil Aviation but then I thought that recently I had become quite notorious regarding the issue of the *kurta-pyjama*. It was better to keep quiet in this society, if one wants to be called civilized, well-behaved, social, cultured and educated.

[8 June, 2003]

# This Social Tie!

The British Airways flight was late by one hour. Standing in the terminal, I was waiting for *Maa* to come out. *Maa*, that is, Dr. Prabha Khaitan.

Very few people know that for the past few years, I have had two mothers, Kusum Bhutoria, who gave birth to me and whom I call Mummy and the one, who gave me life-support, Dr. Prabha Khaitan, whom I call *Maa*.

About five minutes after the announcement of the arrival of the plane, I saw *Maa* coming out of the terminal. I was seeing her after about six weeks and she looked a little weak. I thought that perhaps the weather of Canada and the hectic life of a foreign country had affected her but I was surprised to see that there was not a single line of worry on her forehead.

I asked, "Why, did you keep on worrying about my marriage there too?"

She remained silent. Picking up her luggage from the conveyor belt, she said, "Son, I have hidden something from you. I had some problem in my chest in Canada and after check-up, the left artery of my heart was found to be damaged. I will have to go for a bypass surgery."

I was stunned. When I had talked to her a week ago, she had told me that she had got all the tests done and that I need not worry. In the car, both of us were quiet; she sat silently with her hand on my head.

I soon broke the silence, "Why did you travel in such a condition? You could have called me. I would have come to Canada."

*Maa* said, "Not on the foreign land. On my own land, I..."

After that I could not say anything.

On reaching home, I made a few phone calls. By mid-morning, all the members of the family came to know about her health. Everyone's first reaction was that, if she had come to know of her condition in Canada, what was the need of travelling for twenty-two hours. People go abroad for treatment. She came back from there.

I had to be at the Bhartiya Bhasha Parishad in half an hour, as the secretary of welcome committee for a national seminar on journalism. The Governor, Viren J. Shah was going to inaugurate the programme. I did not feel like going there at all. But *Maa* ordered me, "If you have agreed to it, go. Such is life, it goes on."

No sooner had I come downstairs than I received a phone call from Vishvambhar Newar, "Where are you, Sundeep? You are otherwise so punctual!"

I said, "Just five minutes" and hung up.

Once the programme had started, Acharya Kalyanmal Lodha asked me, "Where is Prabha?" I could not respond. He asked again, "Mohan told me that she had returned in the morning." I nodded. The local editor of the Kanpur edition of *Amar Ujala*, Shambhunath Shukla said, "How come you are late? Has Prabha*ji* come back?" I kept quiet.

I was sitting on the stage but my mind was not there; so much so that when after giving a memento to the Governor, Kishanlal Mahipal extended his hand to shake hands with me, I sat there, quietly gazing at him. Neither did I shake hands properly nor stood up to greet him. He was a bit abashed. The Governor, who was sitting next to me, chastised me saying, "You should have stood up to shake hands with him, he is elder to you after all."

Apologizing to him, I somehow stayed there till the end of the inaugural session and then left saying I had to leave for Jaipur.

It was decided that we should take her to Rabindranath Tagore Cardiological Centre for the check-up and then start further procedure. When at night I told *Maa* that she should not worry, she very calmly but firmly said, "Getting well comes later, I won't even go into the operation theatre till you get married." I laughed it away as usual. The next day I had to go to Jaipur to attend a programme and I had apologized to the organizers saying I would not be able to attend. But *Maa* said again, "No, you must go after accepting the invitation."

I went to Jaipur for the weekend and returned by the last flight on Sunday night. On Monday morning, Dr. Sahu carried out the initial check-up. After a discussion with the famous surgeon of Bengaluru, Dr. Devi Shetty, he said, "Whenever you consider it right, get an angiogram done. Only after that will the exact condition be clear and till then, restrict her speech and movement. She needs rest."

Though the doctor had advised us to admit her to the hospital immediately, *Maa* was adamant that she was all right at home. She could not sleep the whole night on Monday. She asked again, "What have you thought? You should know that if you do not get married, I will not go for the surgery." Tuesday was a repeat of the same sequence of events.

In the evening, Dr. Sahu came. He said, "I am not getting the pulse." Seeing worry on the doctor's face, I also got nervous. The pulse had dropped down to fifty-six and could not be felt anymore. The doctor said that the ECG had to be done immediately. A car was rushed to the nearest pharmacy and the machine was brought.

At night while returning, the doctor said, "I had told you earlier also that she should be admitted to the hospital." At night, I sat silently near *Maa* and then insisted on her going to Bengaluru. She kept on repeating one thing, "Not before your wedding! Either get the bride of your choice or let me look for her. I have had enough. Under whose care should I leave you? You have to decide now. Do what you think is right."

My eyes were moist and I bowed my head in agreement. On Wednesday morning, *Maa* was slightly better. She was sitting on a chair, and was able to leave her bed. She had slept at night. Early in the morning Vinay Neotia came. I was to leave for Bengaluru on Friday to arrange for her operation. *Maa* would come on Sunday night.

Perhaps when you read the next series of *Aapbeeti Jagbeeti* I might be married by then; if not, at least my marriage would be fixed.

If this is told to anyone in a foreign country, they would not believe it. *Maa's* insistence had won. I had no other alternative. Friday evening I had to go. It is late Wednesday night already; that is to say, within the next forty-eight hours I shall have taken a few steps towards tying the knot of marriage.

If my Mummy had been adamant on this issue, I would not have been surprised; a family-oriented Indian housewife's mindset is not to be blamed. But when *Maa*, who is known for her knowledge, wisdom and capabilities, insisted on this issue I was forced to think that the social ties in our country are perhaps above all personal view-points. And the mother of this country is just a mother, whether she is a housewife or an industrialist, or a litterateur or an intellectual!

[15 June, 2003]

# Oh, Society!

Finally I was engaged. Different views of all the family members were expressed. Our society is incomparable in giving advice. During *Maa's* illness, if I had followed the advice of people or had paid attention to the discussion about the doctors, I would have gone mad.

To my displeasure about her coming back without treatment from Canada, *Maa* had a very clear answer, "I had to get you engaged and secondly, my ashes should remain in my own country." She followed what she said, so if I had not agreed to the engagement, she would not have gone to Bengaluru.

In Bengaluru, she was treated by an old acquaintance, Dr. Devi Shetty and she came back to Kolkata with the strict instructions of the doctor. Respecting my wishes, she kept the engagement ceremony simple. She put the ancestral ring on Manjari's finger, put vermilion on her forehead and fed her almond and candy sugar in the temple set up at home; the *roka* was thus completed in the presence of Manjari, *Maa* and I. Besides the three of us, if there was any fourth person present, it was God.

Many of the reforms in our Marwari community do not take place only because everything is presented in the form of meaningless omens and traditions. One puts on such a pitiable face that it looks strange.

"Give as per your capacity. We do not want anything." This has been the tradition of Shankracharya. The issue is that if we did not have this ugly tradition of dowry and pretentiousness; the society would never have considered daughters a burden.

Is it not true that the elderly people, who keep on appealing for social reforms and keep on trying to prove their time was the best, are the biggest blocks in the way of social reforms of young boys and girls?

To tell the bitter truth, all this has hidden selfishness of the families of boys and girls. So much fuss was created on my insistence of not distributing the sweets and the number of good or bad omens that were quoted on my action of sending the sweets back, which was sent by my fiancée, Manjari's family for the first time! I was even given the sobriquet of being mad and crazy. Oh, this society! If you keep on listening to it, it is all yours and you are the respected member of this society; otherwise it does not take any time to point fingers at you.

[22 June, 2003]

# The Show-Off! The Extravagance!

Last week in a prominent newspaper of the city, the details of the celebrations of the ninth birthday of the twins of an industrialist held in a local five-star hotel were published. The birthday celebration was on such a grand scale that about two hundred and fifty people were invited and seventy lacs were estimated to have been squandered on their hospitality. A team from Dubai was called just to present the cake in front of the guests. A renowned pop singer was brought in from Mumbai to sing the songs at the request of the guests on the birthday of the twins. Every half an hour, the look and the theme of the party was changed. While reading the description of this birthday celebration, I was reminded of Bal Thackeray's quote when Rabri Devi was appointed as the Chief Minister of Bihar, "Do I cry or laugh?"

What are these children learning from their parents? It is an extreme case of shamelessness. This is the society that is undergoing the first and the biggest economic recession in the last five decades. But who is going to speak up? If someone speaks, we are with him, but we will not be the ones to raise our voices first. It is everybody's moral duty that instead of looking for the support of the people who speak, one should learn to speak for himself.

The expense of twenty eight thousand rupees on one meal of a person! Perhaps no one has that much money. We all know how money has been collected influencing banks and financial institutions. This may be this gentleman's personal matter but one thing was not personal at all. This spectacle is created to show to the world. And these people, who chortle boastfully, are supported by the papers that narrate such celebrations gloriously.

After my statement against this celebration, I got a call from the office of a prominent English newspaper, "Now it is your turn. Let us see what you do on your wedding." I kept quiet. I thought it was a matter of one or two weeks. He would come to know himself.

I pity the thinking of such people, who spend money on such celebrations, as well as feel sad. Just think how much enmity and jealousy these celebrations create in the minds of people of other castes and communities. Sir, you have lived your life but these children will face the consequences, on the pretext of whose birthday you indulged in this act.

*– Jab kisi gulshan par padti hai, bijli ki nazar*
*Phool si pattiyon par gulaab aata hai*
*Jee me to aata hai ki duniya se baghavat kar doon*
*Lekin uske haath ki chudiyon ka khayaal aata hai* [34]

[29 June, 2003]

[34] When on a garden falls the lightning
Delicate petals turn rosy
I want to rebel against the world
But then I think of bangles on her hands.

# Who Is Right? Who Is Wrong?

In Montreal, one of my business contacts has an organization that holds a prominent place in the business organizations of Canada. The special thing about this organization is that a Jew of Israeli origin and a Punjabi of Indian origin are equal partners.

About two years ago, I had received an invitation for the wedding of the son of this Indian man. I remembered the invitation card because it was singing the praises of the upcoming wedding. The musical invitation gave the details of the parties with eight meals, song and dance programme by a Mumbai group and completely foreign style cocktails and dinner. This wedding was discussed for many days from Montreal to New York, from Chicago to Chandigarh and Delhi.

Last month I received the invitation for the wedding of the son of the Jew partner of the same company through e-mail. It informed about the wedding to be solemnized in the local church on a Wednesday morning.

Though it is a small thing, but it indicated towards a thought process. Here are two equal partners of the same company - a Punjabi, who has three sons and four daughters, spent so much money and must have spent more than two months in all the arrangements; the other, a Jew, who has only one son, completed that work in two hours. Both have settled abroad leaving their own countries. Still why was there so much difference in their mind-sets?

Wedding, the most pious and ancient tradition of our civilization and culture- the first link of family life! Today why has such a pious word become a terror for the father of a girl in our society? Why has everyone made the auspicious occasion of wedding a medium to display one's status and power? How wise is it to squander all the savings of one's life on one meal?

Are those of us who are making an effort to change these futile traditions - wrong? I am not able to judge myself. How is it possible that the five to seven thousand people attending the wedding programmes are wrong and we, the handful of people vying for change, are right?

But it is equally true that for any social change, to start a social movement and a new ideology, not even some, only one person is enough. The morning when you would be reading this *Aapbeeti Jagbeeti*, I would be going through the rituals of marriage in the *yagya-shala*[35] of a local Birla Temple amidst very close family members.

Not even one partner of my vast social and political life is invited. Many people have said that this is wrong on my part. Whether it is wrong or right, the step has been taken; I did not bother about the results earlier nor do I bother about them now. But, I definitely want to express my gratitude to the Birla family, Mrs. Nopani and Pradeep Tandon for their invaluable support for sustenance and success of my ideology, by giving me the permission for holding the first ever wedding in any of the Birla temples in the country, i.e. in Kolkata's Birla Temple.

[6 July, 2003]

[35] The enclosure where fire is burnt as oblation